Testimonials

"Steve has supported our organisation's Agile transformation with all aspects from Enterprise to Squad level coaching, he finds the opportunities, learns the business, and its complexities, to support our people through finding the right way to move forward. This may be through leadership, Alliances of 100+ people, or any other area that influences our people's ability to be more agile. We wouldn't be where we are today without Steve's expertise and support."

Claire Ellison. Head of Transformation,
Marketing Communication, BT Plc

"Working with Steve has been truly refreshing and inspiring. As a Senior Leader he has provided me with the opportunity to really think about the shape of my team, understand the challenges we face and work collaboratively with my people to create a model that works for us and our wider stakeholders. Steve has really taken the time to listen, provide a space for open discussion and has provided invaluable support to me personally and the wider team, providing suggestions on our structure and operational practices to assure our success. There is a genuine excitement and motivation from the whole alliance to adopt a new way of working, driving empowerment and decision-making across the team (not just from the top) as well as learning and development opportunities for everyone. We have the senior support too that underpins our transition to our new working model; allowing us to slow down before we can speed up. I wouldn't hesitate to say that without Steve we would still treading water trying not to sink. Steve is our life raft and we're now steering the ship!"

Leana Keilkowicz, Head of Customer Decisioning, BT Plc

"Working with Steve has helped us challenge the status quo, open our leader's eyes to better working practices and empowered the team to become more creative with their solutions. This transformation has been brought about by a new energy creating improved collaboration, trust and confidence, inspired by Steve's approach through coaching and mentorship. Tough though at times, our leadership team bought into the need for change and with Steve's guidance has created a robust structure with better processes, systems and tools. New roles and responsibilities have been created that make sense of this new Agile world, bringing diversity and growth within the team along with new opportunities for development."

James Day, Decisioning Manager,
Customer Decisioning, BT Plc

"Steve undertook a transformational change and staff development programme with UK Harvest. Steve supported me throughout the journey. I cannot thank him enough for his professionalism, challenge, dedication, direction and time. Steve's input helped change our culture for the better and has secured a positive future for our organisation. I cannot thank him enough."

Yvonne Thompson, CEO, UK Harvest

"Steve was brought in to help our client, National Service Scotland, deliver a new service as part of their response to COVID-19. The two websites, back end and mobile app were to be planned, built and launched in ten weeks.

His excellent Agile skills in coaching the team and leadership ensured the project was delivered on time, providing great value to the customer."

Femke Hawkesworth. Product Manager,
Capgemini Plc

"Steve's versatility and ability to work across different areas of the business; from sales to marketing, product development and operations, together with his patience and ability to drive change in the way we think about building products and working with customers, stands him out."

Peter Forth. Head of Transformation –
Vodafone Business

"Steve provided the right mix of skills, experience and teamwork necessary to make this a very successful project for Pentaho. As this was our first large implementation project, he made a big difference in making this the success that it is. I am not sure we would have pulled it off without him."

Sam Hon. Vice President,
Global Professional Services, Pentaho

Change Starts At the Very Top

Change Starts
At the Very Top

A Simple Guide to Business
Agility Change and Leadership

By
Steve Martin

FIRST EDITION

www.agilistic.co.uk

First paperback edition September 2022

Book design by Publishing Push

ISBNs:
978-1-80227-549-0 (pbk)
978-1-80227-550-6 (e-Bk)

Contents

Acknowledgements

Spanning a career of over 25 years, I am afraid I can't acknowledge all who have inspired me, guided me, and provided me with good work experiences. I would like to give special mention, however, to those that have had a major impact on my working life; To Derren Whitworth and Tim Shaw – just like your favourite teachers, you never forget good leaders. To Iain White – my early-days Agile mentor. To my Agile Coach comrades – Parm Sandhu, Rob Elbourne, Matt Hoskins, Chris Roberts, Raj Kissy and Sean Blezard; I would not be the coach that I am without being challenged by you all with consistent regularity. To my Philips Medical Systems fellows – Ian Chidlow, Richard Jones, Tony Sparrow, Keri Middleton and Jacy Reid. To my many tlmNexus fellows – Martin Barker, Rob Guard, Gavin Fisher, Alex Dawson, David Appleton, Tony Harris, Andy Nelson, Kash Addepally, Chris Fitzpatrick, Peter Simpson, Paul Freer, Steve Marriot, Stewart Caig, Cat McKay, Nic Butler, Mike Veal, Paul Hodges, Phil White, Andy Dobson, Sarah Jackson and of course the switch it off and switch it on again guy; Wayne Henty. To some of my clients; Claire Ellison, Gemma Lavelle, James Day and Leana Kielkowicz (BT), Peter Forth, Lorna Mason, Amit Ghosh, David Townsend, (Vodafone), Femke Hawkesworth, Chris O'Brien, Sharon Bagwell and Ted Euers (HMRC). And the Pentaho data science guys who simply reside on another level of intelligence – Richard Caplin, Mark Stubbs, Mark Robertson, Nelson Souza, Miguel Cunhal, Dan Keeley, Diethard Steiner and Sam Fowler.

Not to mention the other 10,000 people who I have shared a desk with over the years, with whom I have some great memories and from whom I have learnt so much.

Thank you for all your help.

Foreword

Steve has a thirst for learning and coaching teams to be their best! He has a passion for agile and helping leaders and teams make the leap they often don't know they need to make, or how to make! "Change Starts at the Very Top" should be on all leaders TO READ list to act as their bible for how to lead, support and adapt their role in a changing, challenging, competitive and increasing global digitalised world. This book is a key to the door of exceling in the 21st century where the pace of change and customer expectations are higher than ever and barriers to entry lower than ever. His knowledge is second to none and you will find many nuggets of actionable insights and examples to help you fast track your development and expand your leadership or coaching toolkit to help land truly transformation and beneficial change to your teams and customers.

He has been incredibly helpful and taken on many coaching stances in our work together to help me overcome several significant issues or challenges my teams and leaders have been encountering in their transition to greater agility and agile ways of working. We've discussed many thorny issues and come up with a number of paths forward, which have been invaluable to me and proven to be beneficial in making a material change for the better, such as taking on a new stance or running a new experiment to overcome challenges for change.

Darren Mellor
Global Delivery Lead, Lending
HSBC

Introduction

I pretty much spent my early career just coasting from job to job, from company to company, seeking out a career that never really came. I was in the business world which I had always wanted. I was learning so much about everything from Operations to Customer Service, Sales to Marketing as well as the politics and challenges of working within a multi-complex system of people, all synchronised together to get the job done.

It never truly felt like it was working how it should. It always felt like there was something missing – that I was caught up in a world that was falling behind the times. The worlds of fashion, music, media and technology were all racing ahead. But in the world of business, it just seemed like everything was stuck in the Industrial Age, where hierarchy rules and you have to conform with the plethora of reports after reports. The priority was always on profitability, performance and power, with a lot of focus on what the competition were doing, and not enough on what the customer needed and what problems needed solving for them. Success was based on the heights you had climbed rather than the impact you had made, along with the value you had given.

I thought this was how it was supposed to be, but I never truly accepted it for what it was, because it didn't really fit with who I was as a person. I guess that is why I thought it was me that needed to change if I was to fit in.

The problem is, no matter how much you want to fit in (to any culture), it is not that easy if you don't share the same principles of working practices.

It wasn't until I was 14 years into my working life, still searching for my tribe, that I stumbled upon Agile, which was more of an accident than anything else. Having been managing traditional waterfall projects at a small charity for a few years, I had an opportunity to join a local software company as a Project Manager. But in order to secure the role, I needed to take a Scrum Master course. I had no idea what a Scrum Master was at the time. Working in IT was something that had eluded me for most of my career. It was always an area I had considered was beyond my interest levels, but I was strangely drawn towards the ever-growing excitement around tech companies and how they were "taking over" the Universe. They seemed to be disrupting how life had always been in business, and I was eager to get a taste of it.

As soon as we started the course, I was hooked. Everyone seemed to be like me; everything seemed to make sense; it was as if I had come home. I seemed to fit right in. Agile answered questions for me that I had always been asking. Its values matched with mine. Its principles underpinned everything I believed in the business world.

But it wasn't until I started at the software company that things really began to make sense: To see it all happen, and to actually be part of influencing change, to be effective and to be in an environment that was not only dynamic, but where problems were being solved, where there was a clear vision and a unity that I had never seen before.

I hadn't started a new career; I had started a new way of thinking and of working. I was becoming a true asset in a great operation. I was no longer just ticking boxes; I was challenging why the boxes needed to be ticked in the first place with the question being respectfully debated amongst like-minded people – Where was the value?

As I evolved into my new life, I realised all sorts of new wonders and learnt so many incredible things. I still do. But I still cast my mind back to those organisations I'd worked in where they were not using such practices; where the culture was so different, so old-fashioned and I wished they knew what I now know. If only everyone knew then just how much time could be saved, just how effective everyone could become, and just how valuable products and services could be for their customers.

So that is why I created this book to help organisations transform their old ways, to open up possibilities, and also to help provide an understanding of what it is going to take in terms of endeavour, so that you are able to start straight away.

It was over ten years ago that I started my Agile journey, and back then it was all about IT and software practices. Today, it is as much about the organisation; any organisation, company-wide, and regardless of what products and services you have. It's about the culture, the systems, the leadership, and also the customer. Agile is fast becoming standard practice in all sorts of industries, from manufacturing through to utilities. The reason for this is that its main philosophy is all about getting as close to your customer as possible, and being in a position to adapt to changes in needs and demand.

It sounds simple but it really isn't. But what is absolutely vital is that if you are not moving towards becoming an Agile organisation, then you will get left behind. We are seeing on a weekly basis just how brutal the marketplace is today. Huge companies embedded in the very fabric of our society have been obliterated.

Each week, we hear of another company desperate for a bailout, with thousands of jobs lost. The reason for this could be put down to its environment as mentioned before – layers of hierarchy with focus being on profitability, performance and power. But it is perhaps simply that large companies take their eye off the ball, become complacent, lose sight of who they are, where they are going and, most of all, what their customers need. Sometimes they are simply too big to change. Worst of all, they believe they are too big to fail.

It's a really sad sight when you see this happening, and it is happening more and more.

But all is not lost. You are in a great position because you have initiated the first step, by opening this book. Therefore, I would imagine that you at least have a desire to maintain, even go beyond where you are now as an organisation.

This book is a great start for your Agile journey. But you need to have the right mindset. You must be willing to adapt, be willing to take a real step back from your day-to-day operation and have the awareness that in order for you to truly become a successful Agile organisation, you are going to have to lead from the front. Change happens first with

Management. If you show the willingness to your people, then the ride is going to be far less problematic.

Teams cannot change; Individuals cannot change, before Management and Senior Management change. If you are a Senior leader and lack the willingness, or are not fully committed, you may as well stop reading right here, as this book is not for you.

This book will help you with the tools you need to get started. You will be given a roadmap and a strategy on how to become an Agile organisation. You will have an understanding of what is necessary to get there. Taking the time to read this, and building a willingness to change, is going to save you a whole lot of time, energy, and dare I say money later down the line.

From where I first started out all those years ago, to where I have got to now, the world has changed so much. Business has changed, but so have customer demands. As consumers, we are no longer loyal. We expect so much from those that we consume from. We now want speed AND quality. And our minds change a lot. To be successful now in business is not just about how you climb the corporate ladder. It really is about what value you can bring to your customer. And the people with no ego will thrive, simply because it is all about focusing on the customer and delivering value for a greater cause. I may not have known this all those years ago, but I certainly know it now. My hope is that this book will help you not only to build the foundations to create that but also to help change the mindset to allow that; to become a tribe and a culture where those same, like-minded people can truly integrate.

CHAPTER ONE

An Introduction to Business Agility

*"Success today requires the agility and drive to constantly
rethink, reinvigorate, react and reinvent."*

Bill Gates
Business Leader and Philanthropist

What is Agile?

What is Agile? is now becoming an age-old question.
In business, there are so many interpretations and
misunderstandings of what it actually is and what it means.

"Agile is a methodology," claims a Project Manager.
"We're Agile because we are flexible," states an HR Manager.
In my days working with a software company, our main
clients were in the Ministry of Defence. A former RAF
Captain used to tell me that he believed Agile people were
"just a bunch of hippies wearing shorts and flip-flops".

As you can probably imagine, overcoming the opinions of
senior military personnel is the first challenge. Helping them
to reverse centuries of traditional military hierarchy and
command and a control management style, is a complexity

that even someone with my charm and good nature is going to struggle with.

So, let me give you some clarity (or at least the official line) on what "Agile" is, beyond the flip-flops.

Agile is a way of thinking. It is a mindset and a belief. It is made up of 4 values and 12 principles and manifested through an unlimited number of techniques.

Its origin goes back officially more than 20 years, specifically designed for software so that it could move away from the old-fashioned project delivery of long-winded processes, silos and steps. Agility ensures a focus specifically on the customer and that value is delivered early and often.

A group of engineers came together up on a mountain as part of a meeting of minds and with one specific challenge – to speed up the way that software is built and delivered.

What was evident was that building software was taking far too long, with great complexities in more traditional practices. But why was this the case? Why was it being allowed to happen, and might I add, still to this very day as I write, even though Agile practice is becoming standard across organisations in multiple industries?

Could it be down to the old adage that 'this is the way we've always done it"? Could it be that traditional practice was considered safer, that "as long as my bit is done ok then that is all that matters, and I can pass the baton on"? Could it be that having strict processes in place means that we are being very thorough and fully protecting ourselves from risk?. Could it be that any sort of transformation is just too big, complex, risky and costly to do? Or could it be that organisations are too focused on profit, the competition and status rather than transforming how they do things in order to improve the value they deliver to their customers?

The key is very much the customer. With software projects lasting 18 months, sometimes even two years, the world is moving too fast to hang around.

Fundamentally, what was considered valuable today may not be in 18 months' time, and so software delivery was considered too slow and had to change its practices.

But the problem here isn't practice or process. Changing a system isn't necessarily that complex. Obviously, if there are a lot of moving parts it can be, but if everyone is pulling in the same direction then you should be able to do it. What really is the problem is the mindset, which goes back centuries; right back to the industrial revolution when teams were set up based on the required skill. Tasks were set and controlled by Management, and mitigating risk was far more important than delivering value.

The Silos of Developing Traditional Software

Producing new software and making it available for use by the end user requires four key process points: Design – Build – Test – Deliver.

These four stages will always go in the same order in software development, more commonly known as the Software Development Lifecycle (SDLC). Some may argue that in recent times, "testing" has become a lot more fluid in modern software development, i.e., automation test scripts are written alongside designs and run before a single bit of code is cut, proving something will fail before it has begun. So, there is clarity of what needs to be done in order that it will pass. But generally, the four stages are set in stone and will never change.

What needed to change, however, was the number of requirements going through the process.

Historical project delivery relied very much on stages as entire projects or key milestones in themselves. Designers would spend 6 months creating wonderful designs and specifications before throwing them over the fence to the Development Team who would then go and build them. The Design Team would then go and move on to the next project. Meanwhile, the Developers had lots of questions but no one was around to answer them. Six months would pass, and they then threw the project over the fence to the Testers who suffered the same fate as the Developers, and so it goes on. Finally, two years down the road, we finally go live, and the Support Team take on the hot potato.

What a group of engineers realised was that this approach needed to be more dynamic and so came up with some radical thinking.

What they discovered was the need to break down the work; the need to bring skills together to work cross-functionally. There was a need for Designers to work with the Developers who work with the Testers and Integration Engineers. In doing so, they could create a multi-skilled system to solve problems far more rapidly, rather than handing over large-scale projects between teams.

The outcomes would be that they take large requirements, break them down and create them together, as a cross-functional team – Design – Build – Test – Deliver. So, breaking down the silos, no throwing over the fence, and essentially putting all of the responsibility with the team.

As a result, the team can then work closely together to deliver value, often by closing the feedback loop*; they can understand customer needs much more and solve problems continuously. But more importantly, they can adapt to change far quicker than ever before, going from two-year delivery of the entire solution in one hit, down to as little as two weeks for a small, valuable slice of it.

*The feedback loop is the process and length of time it takes to gain feedback from your customer. How tight the loop is, and how adaptable and responsive you are as an organisation, will determine your business agility.

So, this certainly was radical, but it wasn't long before software functions across the world started to see this fairly obvious, yet modern way of thinking and way of delivering software projects.

Nowadays, Agile ways of working have been adopted beyond the software stratosphere and have become a much more cultural way of life in large organisations right through to start-ups.

The cultural perspective is a big one. Simply by allowing cross-functional teams to work together, focusing on the customer and delivering value, it goes further. The softer skills of working together, interacting, listening, respect, trust and even allowances for experimentation broaden out to a company's own values and beliefs. Therefore, decisions can be made faster, teams are more versatile and most importantly of all, organisations can make swift changes.

During the global pandemic, an independent brewery was able to completely change its production line to create hand sanitizer to fulfil growing demand as a result of the Coronavirus outbreak. There is no way that Brewdog would have been able to do this if they didn't have Agile ingrained into their culture and could "design – build – test" and deliver as a cross-functional team to rapidly deliver value.

However, it does have major challenges. Organisations are not so fast to adapt their practices. Companies like Blockbuster, Thomas Cook, Woolworths – organisations that have been around for decades – were unable to respond fast enough to market needs and consequently, they go to the wall.

This is why we are seeing such great demand for expertise. Organisations are now realising that it is fast becoming the industry standard, and their now old-fashioned ways of working just aren't going to cut it in the modern world.

The Two Main Agile Frameworks

Scrum is a disciplined approach to Agile to evolve a product through working closely with the customer, gaining regular feedback, and iterating a solution.

Scrum teams work in short, focused periods of time, which we call sprints, with short-term planning cycles. The benefit here is to keep a sustained pace and bring the customer closely in to collaborate. Each day, the team form a "huddle" to align on progress and raise any issues that are causing delay. At the end of the sprint, the team will review to gain feedback, reflect to raise improvement suggestions on how they are working, and to plan the next sprint. Typically, the sprint will run in two-week increments. The benefit here is that by having short bursts of work, you maintain focus, discipline, and allow for regular interactions with the customer.

Kanban, which translates as "card you can see", is a more flexible approach to Agile which originated in Japan in the 1950s by Toyota, to visualise and manage the process of manufacturing its motor vehicles.

The Kanban operation behaves like a system, and in making it visual for all to see, we can identify really simply where there are areas of the workflow that are being most effective and which ones require the most support and focus. Kanban teams will map their end-to-end process out on a live visible board, and use data to calculate time spent at each step with a view to reducing delays and waste in the system.

In making requirements and tasks small, the system will flow with clear sustainability. Over time, the team will gain predictability which will help with managing stakeholder expectations. This is different to Scrum which uses a timebox to create a rhythm of delivery. Kanban is more of a system that relies on continuous flow and predictability for success.

Both are very effective in their own ways and flexible enough for teams to adapt to fit their preferred working practice. It is becoming far more common nowadays to even combine the two; to have a disciplined structured approach with iterative planning, with a strong focus on optimising the flow of work.

Kanban is widely used in Agile organisations in HR, Marketing, Finance, Operations and, most importantly, senior leadership, with clear visibility and transparency of an organisation's entire workload and strategy.

Why the Need to Go Agile? Why Change?

It isn't really a question of *why* the need to go Agile, but *when*.

We are in the age of disruption, where smaller, nimble, risk-taking companies are taking control and becoming the big players. Twenty-five years ago, there was no Amazon, Google, Netflix, or Facebook. Apple were not the dominant force they are today.

Each of these companies have disrupted their respective industries when there was a chance to prevent them from doing so.

In today's world, profitability and appeasing shareholders are secondary to delivering value. Let's take Blockbuster as a prime example. Back in the 90s, they were the largest retailer of home movies in the world. They were actually exploring streaming services, even before Netflix. So, what happened? They took their eye off the ball, lost sight of what value meant to their customers, lost touch with the marketplace and became complacent. In a little over 10 years, they were gone.

Or there's the high street; large department stores such as House of Fraser or Debenhams, around for decades and really struggling to keep up with a rapidly evolving marketplace. We are no longer using the high street like we used to. Our needs have changed. We can now get most of what we want and need online, therefore, what do we need a high street for? We need radical thinking instead. These types of organisations are not Agile enough to adapt and respond fast.

It's a sorry state and we are seeing it more and more in all types of industries where no one is immune to disruption.

Being Agile is not just about being responsive; it is also about taking risks, innovating, experimenting, testing out ideas and seeing what works for your customers. What happened to Blockbuster? They actually did test streaming home movies. Was it too soon? Did they not innovate enough? I remember in the final years of Blockbuster's existence, going into the shop on a Friday night looking for a movie to watch. I remember thinking that I was being guided through many potential sales opportunities, just like in an amusement park – DVDs, sweets, drinks and popcorn. I would spend over an hour perusing but there was nothing to help me solve my problem –what to watch. That was all I cared about. Blockbuster were focused too much on profitability. When they experimented with streaming, they didn't believe that they could make a profit from it. In fairness, the subscription model had not really become the norm as it is today, and broadband hadn't effectively been rolled out. But even so, had they taken a leap of faith and continued to innovate and experiment, we would be asking what people are watching on Blockbuster now, instead of Netflix.

The high street is going to become much more service-oriented. A place for communities, families and friends to meet and share experiences. Something you can't get online. Department stores should be looking at it from a completely different angle. Identifying the gaps, what needs high street consumers have, and looking at how best to fulfil them, creating a service that you cannot get online.

Agile professionals use these examples a lot; not because they paint a pretty harrowing picture of reality, but because each one of them had the opportunity to change their practices before it was too late. They put profitability over value and took their eye off the ball. They became complacent, believing they had become too big to fail. Nowadays in business, it is not the biggest or strongest company that will survive, but it is the most adaptable to change.

So, to answer the question of why change, fundamentally, it is to increase responsiveness – helping your Product Development and Service Delivery teams to react and adapt to the change in needs of your customers and the market and to increase your speed to market, i.e., breaking down the silos, bringing cross-functional teams together to be able to deliver continuous value. It also allows you to improve the quality of your products and services by getting so close to your customers that you can ensure you are always delivering value to them. As previously mentioned, it creates an organisation-wide focus on "Value". If you are helping your customers understand their needs, solve their problems, and get ahead of the game in foreseeing when those needs may change, you will continue to thrive as an organisation. No company is immune to disruption, as has been proven. But the level of agility you have as an organisation will now determine your future success, and certainly not the level of profitability you have today.

CHAPTER TWO

Key Roles of an Agile Team

*"It is amazing what you can accomplish if you
do not care who gets the credit."*

Harry S Truman
President of the United States 1945-1953

The Role of Scrum Master / Kanban Lead

Traditional Agile teams use a Scrum Master or Kanban Lead
to help them become high-performing. This is the main
objective of the role. Scrum Master is used for Scrum Teams
and, of course, Kanban Lead for Kanban Teams. It is said that
Kanban Teams shouldn't need the services of a dedicated
Kanban Lead as they should be self-organising. However,
I disagree to an extent. I suggest that all teams, especially
those in their infancy, need someone who is focused and
devoted to helping them develop into successful entities. In
the early stages of a team's lifecycle, each member will be
fully focused on their role and also building relationships and
collaborating towards a common goal. It is highly beneficial
for them to have someone making sure that happens. The
role of Scrum Master and Kanban Lead is very similar

with similar characteristics and soft skills, with nuances of difference in the system and operation the team adopts. For the benefit of simplicity, in this part of the chapter, we will focus on The Scrum Master, but the role can easily be adjusted accordingly.

The Scrum Master is the lynchpin of the team; the facilitator, the support, the coordinator, the coach and the one that makes it all happen. The Scrum Master is the driving force behind the team who makes sure that anything that gets in the way of the team's progress is cleared, or even removed for good. Without the Scrum Master doing all they can for the good of the team, the momentum could slow and perhaps even grind to a halt in some places.

The key to the success of an Agile Team is that the Scrum Master is fully engaged and fully focused. In the infancy of the team, it is important for the Scrum Master to be dedicated to the team, as there may be lots of work to be done to get them to a place where they become more and more independent; ultimately becoming a high-performing unit. As time goes on and the team matures, it may become possible for the Scrum Master to step back from being fully dedicated to the team as the team should start to become self-organised.

The Scrum Master needs good negotiation skills. They need to be able to work across multiple levels and departments in an organisation, understanding the needs of not just the team but also the rest of the company as well as the customer. A good Scrum Master protects the team from outside influences. Teams like to poach from each other, especially in times of crisis. This is where the Scrum Master really is influential and uses his negotiation skills to find the best resolution for the customer.

The Scrum Master is a systems thinker and is always looking for ways for the team and its system to improve.

The Scrum Master has no ego. There is no desire to control the team. On the contrary, the Scrum Master takes on a leadership role and serves, ensuring the team have everything they need to succeed.

The more traditional Project Manager may not have some of these characteristics and would be focused perhaps on numbers and reporting rather than customer value and continuous improvement of the team. On the other hand, the Scrum Master uses numbers to identify where the team needs support the most.

Back as a Scrum Master in a software house, I used data as a way to show how much our current server was impacting the team to help upgrade to a new server (the processing speed of our systems was horrendously slow). This was having a great impact on the team and not just from a delay in development where it would take twice the amount of time for anything to get done, but also on morale. My team were becoming increasingly frustrated, and this, of course, impacted productivity. So, the data was crucial here. Just by going to Management and asking for a new server, whilst it was seen as important, it needed to find its place in the pecking order of spend, and that's where the data comes in. Highlight the pain and its impact and it's amazing how fast things can get done.

The Role of the Product Owner

The term Product Owner originates from one that absolutely represents the customer and is therefore fully focused on the needs of the customer. Originally, when Agile first came into practice, it was very much for software development. And therefore, the use of the word "product" is correct. However, as time has moved on and its practice has moved into all areas of the business, in multiple industries, especially those that are more service-oriented, the term "product" is a little misleading. In these instances, as a role, it is still the same but a more appropriate title could be Service Owner. But for now, we will continue to use Product Owner as long as we are all in agreement that it covers both Product and Service, with the onus being on customer representation.

The Product Owner (PO) is the visionary, the one who defines the product's route through its evolution; the one who represents the customer's needs the most; the one who defines the success of the product.

The Product Owner works with the team to help define the right requirements for the customer but also ensures there is a closed loop back to the team to help feedback on the developed product or service.

It is imperative that the PO is solely part of one team. Far too often, I go into an organisation and see the PO spread across multiple teams. This simply won't work (just like the Scrum Master). There are conflicts with time and also with customer needs. The team will need to communicate with the PO regularly, but also, the best use of the PO's time is to analyse data and to stay as close to the customer as possible. This means that they can be fully immersed in the product/ service and its value to the end user, as well as being well ahead should changes in the market occur.

Just like the Scrum Master, this is not a management role. The Product Owner must be a servant leader and help the team have everything they need to develop and deliver a quality product.

Agile for the People

Restructuring an organisation and setting it off on a journey of discovery and change will be both frightening and exciting in equal measure. As leaders, you will have the responsibility to create "containers" for your employees to adapt their own behaviours and working practices in a safe space, with time and freedom to learn and grow.

Your HR team will play a vital role in the transformation, and it will be advisable to include HR representation on the Transformation Team.

One of the major failures of any Agile change programme is the misconception that it is merely a change in working practices. But, as stated throughout this book, people and culture are the driving force behind Agile transformation success. The main responsibility of HR will be to help people navigate their way through the change. They should ensure that people are not left behind, that they feel supported, can create and execute a suitable training and coaching programme for teams, and also establish and embed new roles and responsibilities alongside revised pay and bonus structures. And sadly, an unfortunate inevitability of any transformation programme is that there will be some people who are either not ready or are unwilling to become part of the change. And so, HR co-operation will be required here as well.

Do not underestimate the impact that transformation can have on your people. And also, be very mindful that not everyone will jump in straight away.

Consider the typical way in which we embrace new products as described in The Law of Diffusion of Innovation model, developed by E.M. Rogers in 1962 and which is still relevant today.

The law of diffusion of innovation

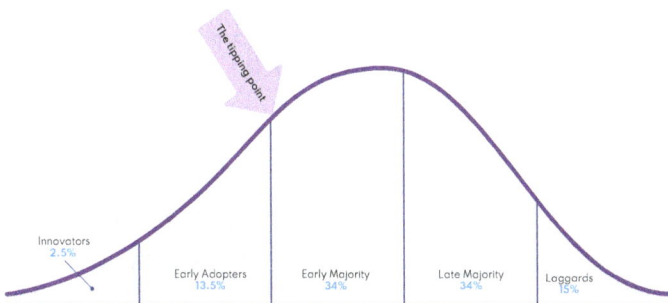

Fig 2.1: The Law of Diffusion of Innovation; EM Rogers, 1962

29

The diagram describes the typical bell curve of buyer behaviour and the tipping point that all companies will strive to reach, where enough people are on board and an early majority can feel safe that the product has been well-validated, creating a natural momentum for growth.

The model can be likened to how people respond to change.

Your innovators will be the ones driving the change, responsible for shaping and creating incubators, safe containers, and structuring the organisation towards Agile success. These are typically Agile Coaches, Change Agents and Transformation specialists.

There will be some who are Early Adopters who will fully embrace the change. They will be like your change champions – the ones who want to be a part of the inception of Agile change, taking any opportunity to learn and adapt. These could well be involved in your Pilot Programmes which you set up at the beginning.

Your Early Majority will be the ones who have seen some benefits already, realise the value and will start to help build on any early success. Enough of these on board will help create your tipping point towards transformation success.

Eventually, your Late Majority will feel left out and have no option but to get on board. But equally, they will be enthused and full of confidence that any promises made at the beginning would come to fruition based on what they would have seen to that point.

Your Laggards sadly may not make it and, for the sake of the success of the transformation, it is vital to identify these as early as possible. They may cause a disruption or a hindrance – even without realising it themselves. Remember, no one comes to work to cause harm. Some are more hard-wired than others, and changing centuries of evolution in the workplace is really complex. It is not for everyone.

Your people will need training, coaching and mentoring on all the various techniques and frameworks available to them. Allowances will need to be made for teams to embed working agreements based on culture and values and how they will work together. They will need to be speaking the same language and be given plenty of space and opportunity to reflect and improve.

Creating Communities Within

Having a sense of belonging and being a part of a community for your employees will really set you apart and not only provide stronger communication lines but will also provide the place necessary for like-minded people to come together, share best practice, formulate ideas, solve common problems and ensure great foundations are built for success of the change.

Typical communities could include:

- Agile Community of Practice
- Scrum Masters
- Product Owners
- Agile Leadership
- Discipline-specific – e.g., *Data Analysts, Design, Technical, Architecture, Product Development, Marketing*

Each will have a clear purpose and be supported in terms of time allocation. You will need these work groups to ensure that you get consistency, effectiveness and efficiencies right across your value streams.

CHAPTER THREE

The Role of an Agile Leader

*"An Agile leader is like a farmer, who doesn't grow crops
by pulling them but instead creates the perfect
environment for the crops to grow and thrive."*
Peter Koning
Author

What is an Agile leader?

To describe an Agile leader, I should probably recap on the behaviours and ways of working of an Agile team. An Agile team have autonomy to make key decisions, work in an environment where they can thrive, are self-organised, are given the space and time to continuously improve to work towards becoming high-performing, and have the right blend of cross-functional skills to deliver value continuously.

The role of an Agile leader is to create the environment for the team to grow and thrive. This includes ensuring the right people/skills, structure, technology, and processes are in place, doing all you can to maximise every opportunity they have to succeed and helping to remove any barriers that may get in their way.

Whilst your Agile teams are self-organising their work, you can then stand back to focus on the bigger picture. We'll look at what that may entail later in the chapter.

The Agile leader isn't simply restricted to Management; we look for leadership skills within the teams themselves. Whilst the Product Owner and Scrum Master/Kanban Lead roles are not Management positions, they still require leadership qualities. The same also goes for technical or subject matter leadership. A good Agile leader will also help to coach and mentor others to be successful.

The original Agile values and principles didn't include anything about leadership. The concept was to evolve over many years. In the early days, and even still today in older, larger organisations, many Managers and Senior Managers feel somewhat lost and become resistant to the prospect of Agile transformation, possibly out of fear, or perhaps simply that there is no distinct role for them. We talk a lot about autonomy and self-organisation for teams. So, if that is the case, where does that leave Management?

In fact, all the theory behind Agile looks more toward teams and how close they can get to their customers and disregard the role of the more traditional manager. Consequently, what we then get faced with is a half-baked attempt at change, possibly because Management don't really feel it is for them, but do appreciate the need for their teams to do so.

However, this could not be further from the truth, and with this being the subject matter of the book, it's the greatest misconception that people can have about Agile practices.

Whilst there is not a dedicated role in Agile for Management, it is the behaviour and management style that needs to change to enable success of its practices amongst teams and customers. And, as mentioned earlier in the book, Agile requires a mindset shift, which is the most complex of changes to make – and if you are already doubtful of the benefit to you as a Manager, because of the team focus, fearful of what is involved, that you may be put at risk without a role to hold onto, then you will be less likely to take the leap of faith and join your colleagues on the journey and fully embrace the change.

I'm not going to pull any punches here – the transformation will succeed or fail based on your own willingness and mindset. You have a responsibility to lead the change, become a champion of Agile practice, develop transparency with a willingness to show your vulnerability, to help build trust and to change your management style for the greater good of the organisation's capacity to succeed as an Agile organisation.

So, there is absolutely a role to play in the transformation, but what about your role as a Manager and leader in the new world?

The Role of an Agile Leader: Set the Vision – Look Beyond the Horizon – Measure Value Outcomes – Support the Team

Set the Vision:

When US President John F Kennedy visited the NASA Space Centre in 1961, he was introduced to various staff and representatives there who all had a part to play in the greatest mission that the world had embarked upon to that point. As he went along the line, he was greeted by a variety of workers, all keen to meet the President and give an account of their job. He eventually came to a humble caretaker. "And what is it that you do?" asked the President, for perhaps the 20th time in the line. "I'm helping to put a man on the moon," replied the caretaker.

The caretaker had separated his job from his role. His job was a means to an end, to be paid a wage, to look after his home and family. But his role was to contribute to the mission, and it was that clearly defined vision that kept him motivated to work. He knew that if he looked after the station and kept it clean and in good working order, then the rest of the team could move one step closer.

Every employee, from the astronauts and engineers to the secretaries and interns, was so singularly focused. "Even people who were quite far removed from the famous goal of landing a man on the moon reported feeling an incredible connection to this ultimate goal," wrote Andrew Carton, a Professor of Management at The Wharton School, University of Pennsylvania in his inductive investigation of the lunar landing.

The vision was clear, and it came right from the top.

JFK stood before Congress in May 1961 and set out a commitment to put a man on the moon before the end of the decade. It inspired a generation of Americans, and the role of the President was to provide everything necessary to make it happen.

Your vision for the company, or product or service doesn't need to be something as adventurous, but it absolutely must inspire, be ambitious yet achievable, and have a clear and tangible purpose.

In 2013, Netflix CEO Reed Hastings released an 11-page memo to employees and investors detailing a commitment to move from just distributing content digitally to becoming a leading producer of original content that could win Emmys and Oscars.

As the memo said, "We don't, and can't, compete on breadth with Comcast, Sky, Amazon, Apple, Microsoft, Sony, or Google. For us to be hugely successful, we have to be a focused, passion brand. Starbucks, not 7-Eleven. Southwest, not United. HBO, not Dish."

Since unveiling that new purpose, Netflix's revenue has roughly tripled: its profits have multiplied 32-fold, and its stock has increased 57% annually.*

The vision statement is important and will have a different perspective for employees, shareholders, and customers. Even more powerful is the mission statement to underpin the vision. It is important to appreciate where you are at now, accepting the position you are in and showing accountability and responsibility for where that position stands and showing honesty to your people. Here is an example of what a vision could look like for an Agile Transformation...

We understand that, as an organisation, the way we work does not always account for the most effective or efficient

* Source: Harvard Business Review

processes in how we best serve our customers. We know we have not always got things right and that we have made mistakes. We know that the culture of the organisation needs some work to develop the sort of trust necessary to ensure accountability throughout.

The future of the organisation is really exciting for we are going to transform to become much more Agile in our practice, more responsive to our customers' needs, create a culture of innovation and that everyone in the company will embark on this challenging, yet thrilling journey. This won't be for everyone, and that is ok – we bear no ill will and wish you well for the future. But if you are willing and committed to working with us and having the patience to see this become a real success, then you will have a great opportunity to be part of something really special.

For people to have a sense of belonging, to be a part of something special, to really get behind it, the vision needs to have authenticity and a genuine acceptance that everyone, from the highest level through to the teams on the ground, will be embarking on this journey. It must also be made clear that whilst there will be challenges ahead, and some pain, we will tackle them together as we go.

What shape do you want the organisation to become? How much autonomy are you willing to give? What structure will you set out? What is the measure of success? These are considerations to iron out as part of the strategy.

Look Beyond the Horizon:

With your vision in place, and in putting the trust in your teams to focus on the immediate needs of your customers, delivering value early and often and ensuring the feedback loop is tight enough to be fully responsive, in turn, paves the way for you as a leader to focus beyond the horizon. What is the high-level strategy to enable teams to fulfil your vision? What is coming down the track? What could be happening in future markets that may impact on your strategy? What market opportunities are there?

If you are too focused on the immediate progress of your teams, you will lose sight of the road ahead. Keep an eye out, yes, and be there to support, but focus instead on the future.

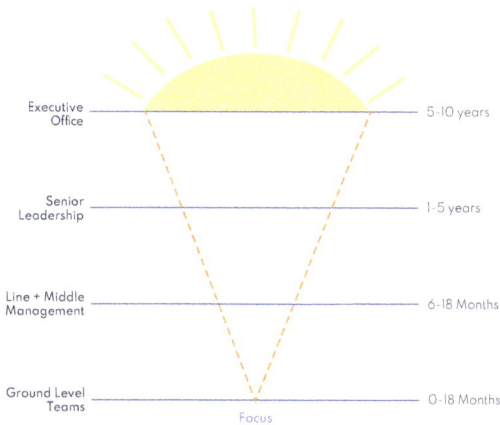

Executive Office		5-10 years
Senior Leadership		1-5 years
Line + Middle Management		6-18 Months
Ground Level Teams		0-18 Months

Focus

Fig 3.1: Leadership Focus

Executive Office (5–10 year view)

- find the right business strategy that works for the entire organisation, setting out the path for success
- research future technologies and business practices
- continuous organisational agility focus

Senior Management (1–5 Year View)

- find the right market strategy that works for the division in line with overall business objectives, setting out the path for success

41

- research future technologies and business practices
- continuous cross-functional division agility focus

Line and Middle Management (6–18 month view)

- find the right operational strategy that works for your teams, setting out the path for success
- market trend analysis and forecasting
- support the team; (Resources, tools, environments, process)
- continuous multi-team agility focus

Product Development / Service Delivery Teams (0–18 month view)

- continuous delivery of value
- behavioural analysis to understand changes in needs
- tight feedback loop
- continuous team improvement

Measure Value Outcomes – OKRs

Everything that an organisation does should be directly linked to the value that it provides to its customers.

And it must be measurable, not only to support prioritisation of new requirements, but mainly to identify changes in customer needs.

Key Performance Indicators – KPIs are most commonly used to demonstrate how effectively a company is performing against its objectives, usually linked to financials, operation or customer satisfaction. KPIs have been used since the industrial age, when individuals operating rudimentary tasks could be accurately measured.

However, in today's world, where behaviour, emotion and value are very difficult to measure, we need a different method to gauge success.

But how do we know the level of success attributed to value? How do we know how well our people are doing? How do we know that the work that we do is having a positive impact? Traditional organisations are very good at setting out targets and objectives, but rarely are they connected to value.

1-Click to Measure Value

When Amazon introduced its 1-Click solution, it was to change the world of e-commerce forever and allowed them to gain a strong foothold in the marketplace, transforming

Amazon from an online bookstore into the multi-faceted superpower that we now know.

Today, we think nothing of automated field-filling, with names, addresses, and credit card numbers in storage, and called into action on demand, to make the process of purchasing online, on our mobile phones especially, as seamless as if we were physically in the shop handing over our payment cards. But back in the early 2000s, we were not so trusting. We had not even moved away from using chequebooks, and cash was still the most trusted way to spend.

The problem that Amazon and many other eCommerce stores were facing was that the level of revenue lost at the checkout was just too high. Amazon realised that in order to overcome this problem, they needed to focus on improving the end-to-end customer journey from product search to payment, to delivery, creating a swift and seamless experience for its customers, fundamentally reducing the time and effort it would take to make a purchase.

The objective, therefore, was clear, but the **how** required a change in culture for its customers: there was a need for complete trust in the storing of personal data. And it didn't happen overnight. It did take a number of years for the trust to build, and eventually, that is exactly what happened.

Amazon's **Measurable Outcome** was to reduce the level of lost revenue at the point of sale caused by Abandoned Shopping Carts. Part of the solution would be to give customers the ability to make one click and the purchase and delivery are made.

It is unknown whether the teams involved in the solution came up with the idea for 1-Click. However, when teams and their leaders are creating Objectives and Key Results (OKRs) with Measurable Outcomes, I always encourage that those closest to the product or service should be given the opportunity to come up with their own ideas to help influence the success of achieving the OKR target measure. The level of motivation created by giving autonomy to Agile teams in being in control of their own success cannot be understated.

The main advantage of Amazon's 1-Click was the level of value attributed to its customers. Reducing the effort in entering personal data each time would save time and energy for users and therefore increase demand for its products.

And value is what we focus on in running OKR Measurable Outcomes workshops with Agile teams, leaders and stakeholders.

The standard process is to get everyone together in the same room and firstly establish the main purpose of the team or organisation, focusing in on why the team or organisation exists, what problems they solve for their customers and what value they deliver. We look at who are the customers and where are the touchpoints of a team or organisation's products and services?

The problems to solve and value are then prioritised based on importance and level of impact before we look at success criteria of solving problems and ways to measure.

There are 6 key factors involved in creating quality OKRs:

1. *Measurable*: They must have a baseline (what is the measure today?) and everyone in the room sets and agrees on a realistic target to aim for.
2. *Simplicity*: It's important to keep the number of objectives to about three for simplicity and focus. I've worked with a number of different teams and organisations where they might have a whole list of objectives to work with. But typically, they tend to confuse solutions with objectives and therefore we will take it up a level and find it comes out to about three solid objectives.

3. *Team Control:* Teams must have direct influence on achieving their OKRs without dependency. Any objective where they are reliant on another team will reduce the capability of the team to reach the OKR and consequently reduce the level of motivation to succeed.

4. *Complete Alignment:* With the team, Management and stakeholders in the room together, then everyone is aligned to the OKRs and therefore the Product Owner can use these as the primary criteria for prioritising the work.

5. *Review Regularly:* It is important to regularly review the OKRs as things do change. I would always suggest a 3-6-month interval, or if targets have been met, whichever comes first. The flexibility to review regularly allows for stakeholders to be satisfied that the customers they represent are always getting the highest value possible.

6. *Visibility and Live Status:* Ensure that there is clear visibility of the live status of each of your teams' and organisation's OKRs to help with motivation, identify where support may be required and also help show a real-time level of value that you are delivering to your customers.

Once OKRs have been set, we then review the Product Backlog and come up with ideas as to how we can achieve the agreed targets. This part of the process is always slightly controversial as the question becomes, "does it help us to fulfil our OKRs?" If the answer is "no" then it should be deprioritised.

And this is why it is essential that we have alignment across the organisation, as there will be stakeholders not particularly keen that their requirements are dropping down the list.

So, now you will be getting into a much stronger position because you will be using key measurables to question why you are doing something perhaps believed to be the most important initiative.

And that will be part of your role as an Agile Leader; to protect the team from the pushback and support them to reach their Measurable Outcomes.

Support the Team

The final part of the role as an Agile Leader is to support the team; to clear everything out of the way that is preventing progress by way of managing an escalation system as mentioned earlier in the book:

People: Ensure the right skills and capability for the team to deliver the right value continuously.

Process: Help support changes in process to ensure continuous value delivery and rapid response capability for your teams.

Technology: Work tirelessly to enable the very best technology is in place to support continuous value delivery and rapid response capability.

Structure: Set up for success by structuring teams to get as close to your customers as possible without the need for handoffs to 3rd parties and approvals.

However, the support also goes further, especially during the phase of transformation. People need the space and capacity to change the way they work together as well as transform the way they think. As leaders, you have a responsibility to enable the space and capacity and help protect them from outside demand and be mindful of any pressure put on them due to misunderstandings of the capability increase of Agile practice. High-performing teams should have greater capacity to increase workload, but this takes time and allowances will need to be made for teams to reach this level.

You cannot change the tyre on a moving car. The level of commitment for delivery will have to drop as teams settle and adjust their working practices. And you can support that by providing the guard rails necessary to help protect teams from the pressure being piled on them by your stakeholders and that ensure everyone is pulling in the same direction.

There needs to be an awareness that change is complex, and takes time, effort, and most of all, space. Setting expectations that the same level of output is expected during the transformation period is simply going to cause greater harm than good, and regrettably you may find that good people will either leave, or the level of quality in your products or services is likely to diminish.

At BT Consumer – A drop in delivery commitment had to happen for there to be success in transforming their Customer Decisioning Alliance (CDA). Firstly, the leadership team of CDA had to put the case forward to their Senior Leadership Team – mapping out value-based work that was to be de-prioritised. Then difficult conversations needed to happen with the wider stakeholders on the commercial steerco. The reaction was really positive. Simply by bringing those effected into the conversation and providing a clear picture as to what was happening and helping everyone to understand the purpose, provided a great sense that CDA were in control, had a good plan and strategy and that the benefits of the change would be far far greater than what they were used to.

And the reaction from the Alliance was really positive too. Employee churn rates dropped and the morale and motivation increased. The change took some time but they were well on their way within weeks and therefore their stakeholders could realise value far sooner.

So, support your teams by ensuring there is a sufficient level of time and space for transformation to happen, and be patient. The rewards for Agile implementation will be reaped in time.

Behaviour and Mindset of Agile Leadership

Good leadership is not necessarily associated with being Agile specific, but the types of characteristics fit quite nicely with Agile practices. The more traditional command-and-control leadership style where authority, stature and decision-making are prevalent, tends to hinder the progress of Agile teams in becoming high-performing. This style of

Management does not lend itself too well to Agile practice, where you are putting your trust and faith in those closest to your customers to crack on whilst you take care of the bigger picture. If you are more familiar with being involved and more hands on as a Manager, this is going to be a real challenge for you. You feel you need to be in amongst the action to be able to influence, maintain control, provide the necessary support needed, and be able to communicate across other areas of the business.

The modern age of industry requires creative thinking to solve problems, and moves away from traditional task-oriented delivery processes, where the command-and-control style would have been much better suited. This particular style focused teams on the importance of output and results. Modern Agile organisations instead focus on outcomes and value. Therefore, a style better suited to creative thinking and innovation is required.

A Servant Leader. A leader who is a servant first and ensures that the needs of their team are being met.

A Servant Leader:
- works tirelessly to develop his/her people.
- Is focused on what they can do for others.
- empowers people to be the best they can be.

- removes impediments for his/her team so that they can do their job and do it well.
- challenges the status quo.
- encourages clarity and competency.
- helps people develop and highly perform over asserting power.

The Servant Leader puts others first. They see their own role as being to help others develop and perform as well as possible.

In his book, 'Turn the Ship Around', Captain David Marquet describes how his style of barking orders and command-and-control resulted in poor performance and low morale in his crew.

One of Marquet's observations was that he was the one with all the power and the only member of the crew with the responsibility to make every decision on the vessel. Not one of his crew was empowered, and therefore, they were not given the autonomy to think or act for themselves, or for the benefit of the crew. They were working in a culture of fear and lacked the motivation to work together as a team.

He explains that for this to change, his own style had to change and demonstrates how the style of Servant

Leadership was so effective in transforming the culture and behaviour of the US Navy Nuclear Submarine, the USS Santa Fe, which subsequently went from being the worst to the best in the fleet. In fact, in the second year of the transformation, they scored the highest grade that the inspection team had ever seen.

This level of change in leadership style requires great self-awareness, willingness, and commitment, and we tend to see one of two things happening to Management in organisations going through a transformation.

1. **Resistance to change** – Being resistant is a psychological response and not necessarily a conscious one. It will involve an element of being in denial of change not being necessary – though this could well be. But also, in denial that as a Manager, you are responsible for leading the change; instead, leaving it to the teams you are managing. Being resistant will naturally then reflect on your people. They will see that you are not on board and will instead become resistant themselves. They will also be confused as to what they are supposed to be doing, and possibly afraid to push back against a way of working that doesn't fit with how they have been asked to work. This can cause major

damage to the transformation. Unfortunately, it is all or nothing. You cannot be supportive of the change but at the same time resistant. It will have a knock-on effect and you won't see it until it is too late.

The sorts of resistant behaviour or anti-patterns to look out for could be as simple as carrying on your working practice, requesting regular information through reporting, having regular meetings to delegate tasks, disregarding the importance of team ceremonies like daily stand-ups and retrospectives in place of your own agenda, and a general refusal to show your own transparency through the visibility of the work you are doing during the transformation period.

2. **Lead the change –** Alternatively, we see Managers step into a position of Servant Leadership, identifying their position in the transformation and doing whatever they can to make it a success, leaving the ego at the door, and showing a real willingness and commitment to lead the change.

Fundamentally, they make great allowances for change to happen, protecting teams from outside influence and internal politics that can scupper progress and supporting the team to give them everything they need, clearing the way towards high performance.

Self-awareness is essential here. Don't be afraid to take some time out to look inwardly at your own leadership behaviour and be honest with yourself about how much willingness and commitment you are prepared to give to make the transformation a success. How much control are you willing to offset to your people in order to create self-organised, sustainable, and high-performing teams? What sort of leader do you want to be in this new world? And most importantly, how can you show your own vulnerability to build trust and strengthen relationships with your people?

You will need to be really mindful of just how your own behaviour and leadership style is impacting your people and whether you are unconsciously hindering progress.

Part of your role as an Agile Leader is to create a mechanism for your people to stop looking inwards to serve the leader and move towards a culture where they look outwards to serve the customer.

I'll leave this section with a bit of food for thought, as this is the most important part of the book – mindset and behaviour are everything, especially in transformation. Both myself and a fellow Agile Coach Parm Sandhu once gave an 'Agile for Leaders' training session to a large group of multi-level Managers for a medium-sized utilities company based in the UK. They were embarking on an Agile Transformation. It was a remote session and so the level of control we had to make sure everyone had their cameras on, were fully engaged and focused, was limited. Three days before the event, we were asked for two things;

i) could we provide a detailed breakdown of each section so that each Manager could decide which ones could be relevant to attend?

ii) could we split the sections into 3 x 2-hour blocks for each day so that each Manager could work in some meetings in-between and therefore maximise their time?

This was a sign.

They were not fully committed to the training, and possibly the transformation.

We were also told that both the Head of Customer Experience and the CTO were going to "dip in and out". Sidenote: the CTO was the sponsor for the transformation, and basically the reason we were there in the first place!

Overall, the training went okay, but the biggest problem was the level of engagement throughout. The same people would speak up time and again, very much the ones on camera. What was evident was that those that were not engaged were handling urgent issues away from the training. We were even told that during day two, the CTO had called a few of them away from the training for an unrelated call.

Would any of this have happened onsite and face to face? Possibly not, but even so, the behaviour and mindset of Management was clear and disruptive.

Parm and I continued to coach teams and leaders over a 3-month engagement but we were becoming increasingly excluded from key management strategy sessions.

Not long after our engagement had come to an end, we were informed that the company had cancelled the transformation altogether and some Management had been made redundant. It was explained that the organisation had considered Agile and realised it wasn't for them.

Sadly, this sort of scenario happens a lot, and is the reason I am labouring the point here. Had there been a stronger commitment, greater focus, and REAL Agile leadership, the company would have made a great success of the change.

CHAPTER FOUR

The Agile Culture

"Doing agile is a set of activities, but being agile is the state of mind, the ongoing capability, and the cultural adaptability."

Pearl Zhu

Author, Innovator

The Blame Game

Our politicians are world champions at deflecting responsibility. Imagine a world where a Member of Parliament stands up and says...

"I am sorry. I got it wrong. But I have learnt from my mistake, and next time, I will do things differently."

How much respect would we have? The media wouldn't know what to do. The opposing parties wouldn't know what to do. They would all be looking around asking the question, "Is this how it is now? Is this how we are supposed to be?" Well, yes!

Think about how much more powerful it would sound if a whole group stood up and said, "We got it wrong".

Why don't politicians ever say sorry? Why don't they take accountability and responsibility for their decisions?

Why don't they accept that they got it wrong? Yes, they will apologise on behalf of a historic event, where their position as a Member of Parliament is not under threat.

In 2010, the then UK Prime Minister, Gordon Brown, apologised to the family of World War II Enigma codebreaker Alan Turing on behalf of the British Government. In 1952, Turing had been sentenced to chemical castration for being gay and subsequently took his own life two years later, aged just 41.

Alan Turing was a mathematical genius and the person whom we have now come to know as being responsible for shortening the war by as much as two years through his construction of the Enigma Machine. The story, as well as Turing's life, was kept top secret for almost 40 years.

Prime Minister Gordon Brown claimed, "We're sorry. You deserved so much better". This statement proves nothing more than simply accountability is far easier when it is on behalf of a historic event.

When we are small children and misbehaving, such as when we accidentally push over another child, we are told, "Say sorry and they will forgive you". Your gut wrenches with fear and anxiety. You say sorry and hold out a hand. And then what happens? The other child will say, "That's okay. Thank you" and responds with an open hand for you to shake. And then you run off and carry on playing together, but just that little bit tighter as friends; a little more respectful of each other.

Or what about when you broke something and you blamed it on your sister; you almost got away with it even though the evidence was clear to see as you had the dust all over your t-shirt. The punishment was firm, not because you broke something, but because you did not take responsibility for your actions. You tried to place the blame on an innocent party. Did you do that again? Probably, yes. Was the punishment insufficient the first time around?

Passing blame is one of the worst traits in a human being, and collectively, it can be like a cancerous disease that spreads throughout a team and an organisation, causing mistrust, anxiety and fear. If you have a blame culture, you can actually feel it as you walk through the door. There is tension in the air; whispers in the corridor. People are too afraid to speak. And that fear builds up to such a degree that it can completely stifle innovation.

Imagine a software engineer in the early stages of their career – Fresh. Hungry. Full of energy – and during an exercise to completely revamp a new server environment, they accidentally delete a really important file. Now, one of two things could happen. First of all, they can be chastised and ridiculed; shown up in front of all of their colleagues, taken off that task and put on another with lesser risk. Or, as a team, you could come together and accept that actually maybe it isn't anyone's fault, and instead, explore why it was so easy to make a mistake in the first place. Perhaps it was by not having a trigger in place, like a warning to flag up to prevent key files from being removed. Or maybe having a recovery system to ensure that certain files are kept safe somewhere before being permanently deleted.

If that Engineer is chastised and humiliated, what do you think will happen to their confidence? How do you think they will feel about it? How will it look to the rest of the team, or even the organisation? What message does it send to everyone? Who will they ask next time to get involved in a high-risk task? Certainly not the Junior Engineer. What happens when they go home that night feeling low and despondent? How will they feel about the company they work for?

Imagine their confidence when realising that "<u>the system</u>" is what needs to be fixed and that, as a team, there is collective responsibility to fix it; coming up with ideas on how to prevent such an error from happening again. They are then given the task of taking ownership of that idea to see it through. Their energy levels will be surging. You will have just ignited their spirit and they will go home that evening feeling proud, responsible, and highly motivated.

Which type of company would you prefer to be a part of?

As humans, we don't go to work to be malicious or wishing to break things. We don't consciously intend ill-will on others. We all wish to make a success of what we do. Most people will want to do the best job that they can. So, when we are guilty of blaming others, all we are doing is destroying confidence, losing trust and deflecting responsibility. And if that is the culture, then all that is happening is that you are slowly "turning out the lights" and you will subsequently lose all of the good people in your organisation.

In Agile, there is no blame. There is collective account-ability and responsibility in everything that we do and at every level. We look at the system to be fixed and we ensure that there is room for those less competent to enhance their skills, knowledge and experience through mentorship and training.

"Regardless of what we discover, we understand and truly believe that everyone did the best job they could,

given what they knew at the time, their skills and abilities,
the resources available, and the situation at hand."

Norm Kerth, Project Retrospectives
Author, *A Handbook for Team Review*

Having a culture of blame is the most important element of your organisation that you must eradicate from the outset of your Agile transformation.

If you are unaware that you have a blame culture, then next time one of your managers comes up to you to complain about something or someone, do a little investigating and see if there is simply a deflection of responsibility at play.

Innovation is the Key to Sustained Agile Success

"Creativity is the ability to create new and potentially valuable ideas in any activity.
Innovation is the process of transforming these ideas into a commercial reality (i.e., testing, measuring, learning & sharing)". Dr Ken Hudson

Organisations that value and encourage innovation, i.e., where it is okay to fail and learn in order to succeed, will always be one step ahead of those that are more risk-averse.

Innovation doesn't happen in a small section of the business, in a lab environment. Innovation should be embedded into practise across every aspect of the company. Agile organisations embrace the ethos that failing is okay as long as you learn and adapt.

Agile teams that are given the freedom to be creative and innovative, will experiment in real-world conditions where they can work with their customers to establish what works and doesn't work. With tight feedback loops, teams can then evolve a product or service, ensuring that they are solving problems and creating the best, most valuable solutions.

Measuring feedback is vital, even by including Business and Data Analysts within teams, to be able to help study results, as in any science experiment, then using these results to create quality products and services.

And innovation means only making minor improvements to an existing product or service to enhance its effectiveness, efficiency, and value.

Twenty years ago, we wouldn't have dreamt we would all be so reliant on smartphone technology. But the evolution of the Apple iPhone has led us to demand hi-tech features such as facial recognition, geo-satellite location finders or AI-driven personal assistance. Not to mention music players, social media, internet search and about a million different applications to assist you in just about anything. Oh yes, and a phone and text service – the mobile phone's original function. It's incredible really that we still call it a phone.

Innovation has been the driving force behind the evolution of Apple's iPhone ever since v1.0 back in 2008, and it is engrained into each of its Product Development Teams to keep being creative and striving for excellence.

Organisations that consider innovation as a costly luxury tend to be more focused primarily on driving profits over value.

Going back to my concern for the demise of the high street that I mentioned in Chapter 2, we can see what is happening, and it could so easily be avoided. If large department stores changed their culture to take some risks, to experiment and to try to innovate the type of service they provide to the walk-in customer, there may well be a chance they could survive, and even thrive.

Could they put a couple of teams together with a remit of experimenting with a new way of shopping on the high street? Could they gather a focus group of customers to understand requirements and test out some different solutions? Could they make greater allowances and give autonomy to innovate, with a clear message that it is okay to fail, as long as you can learn and adapt? Could they be given sufficient time to revamp the entire end-to-end experience?

I mentioned at the beginning of this book that Agile practice is primarily a mindset; a way of thinking. Changing it is the most complex challenge that any organisation will face. However, the rewards far, far outweigh the distress that you must go through to transform the entire company. You can't do these things half-measured without a complete change in culture.

Continuous Improvement Towards High Performance

Innovation should not be restricted just to product development and service delivery.

Agile organisations, and specifically Agile teams, are always looking for ways to adapt their processes to become more efficient, more effective and most of all more sustainable. By getting closer to their customers, they are able to identify feedback and likely changes, but now have the culture to adapt accordingly.

It is important to mention here that when we talk about continuous improvements, we are not talking about strategic change from above. Continuous improvement should be considered a tactical change that takes place during the flow of work. Yes, taking time out occasionally to review and reflect is essential. But Agile teams take a systemised approach on a daily basis, using key data points as well as members of the team, to help identify where tweaks need to be made.

To define how continuous improvement is essential in building high-performance teams, we can use the example of an Olympic Indoor Cycling team. The difference between the top five national teams at Olympic level is so fine that to set themselves apart to become champions, they must look at the smallest detail to determine where they may be able to gain an advantage.

When Dave Brailsford became Performance Director of Team GB Cycling in 2003, he introduced the theory of marginal gains as a strategy to create a culture of continuous improvement, with a true vision – to put the team at the very top and keep them there for many years.

He believed that if the team could make 1% improvements in every aspect of the team, then the athletes could significantly improve results.

Brailsford and his team looked at the entire make-up of the athlete's lifestyle; from the amount of sugar in their diet, to the amount of sleep they were getting each night, to fitness conditioning levels, through to specific details on personal happiness, focus, concentration, and energy. They focused right in on the equipment they used, redesigning the bike seats to make them more comfortable and rubbing alcohol on the bike tyres for a better grip. Riders wore heated shorts to maintain ideal muscle temperature while riding and used special data sensors to monitor how each athlete responded during fitness sessions. The team tested various ways in which to increase clothing to become aerodynamic. They tested different types of massage gels to see which one led to the fastest muscle recovery.

The lengths to which the team went even involved travelling with special bedding and mattresses to every destination, to ensure athletes could sleep in the same position everywhere they went.

Everyone responsible for the support of the team, from the team bus driver through to the Head Coach, was aligned on how they were going to become Olympic champions.

Brailsford described the marginal gains approach: "The whole principle came from the idea that if you broke down everything you could think of that goes into riding a bike, and then improved it by 1%, you will get a significant increase when you put them all together.

"We had three pillars to our approach, which we called "the podium principles." The first one was strategy. The second was human performance; we weren't even thinking of cycling, but more about behavioural psychology and how to create an environment for optimum performance. The third principle was continuous improvement."

Under Brailsford's leadership, Team GB led the cycling medal table at the 2008 and 2012 Olympic Games, winning eight golds at both, whilst British cyclists won a total of 59 World Championships across different disciplines from 2003 to 2013. Brailsford then led Team Sky to six victories in seven years at the Tour de France.

Now, a typical Product Development or Service Delivery team may not need to test out which clothing material is going to make them more aerodynamic in the way they work together; nor may it be necessary to bring their own mattress from home when travelling overseas for a work meeting in order to maintain consistent sleep patterns. However, having a clear focus, desire, and, most of all, time to make incremental improvements will be the key ingredient towards becoming a high-performing unit.

Some mature Agile teams adopt a Kaizen approach, a technique originating in Japan, where they identify a 1% improvement every day, a small change. That will come, given the right support – but to start with, make sure you are giving sufficient slack in the system for teams to regularly reflect and identify improvements on how they work together; their systems and processes, and even learning needs. Allow them the freedom to experiment with different processes to find the one that is most effective and efficient, measure the impact and continuously adapt. Doing this on a regular cadence will enable great maturity to happen at pace.

Traditional organisations are set up in a way where improvements or innovations are stifled because the level of responsibility is not given to the team. Any improvements are required to go through a scrutinised hierarchical process with higher-level Management to reduce any risk. Sadly, because of this, teams will be reluctant or fearful of making improvements, because the process is too complex or long-winded. Consequently, they will simply carry on doing what they have always done and get the same results they always get. To continue the analogy further, it would be like the Management of an Olympic cycling team simply sending riders out on their old bikes and scruffy kit with the expectation that they have enough to win gold.

Trust and Respect are the Foundations for High Performing Teams

Embedding a philosophy of continuous improvement and experimenting with new ways of working, measuring, learning and adapting will not be possible without creating a culture of trust and respect, where cross-functional teams and Management can work in unison for the good of the customer, and following one vision for the company.

It sounds so simple, doesn't it? You would be amazed at how many companies and teams I come across where there is a fear of failure, and where the complex hierarchy of Management control the reins of responsibility too tightly. There is no experimentation because the demand is so great that there generally isn't any time or slack in the system to do so. And even if there was time, the risk of failure is too great.

How can a team grow into a high-performing unit if they can never be given the trust to improve how they operate together?

If they are not trusted by Management, how can they trust each other?

Trust has such a powerful and fundamental influence on an organisation's success, and a lack of trust can be equally detrimental.

A great sign to look out for in your teams is to see how ideas or suggestions are taken on and implemented. If a less experienced member of the team makes a suggestion that is shot down by a more experienced member of the team, it is fairly clear that there is a trust and respect issue.

That team member may not risk being shot down again and you would have lost them forever.

When you start out in a new relationship, trust is expected but it doesn't really exist until you get to know each other. We assume trust is all about cheating; that you trust that they will be loyal to you and not have eyes elsewhere... or worse. But it is actually far deeper than that. Trust of a partner means that you can tell that person anything and they won't judge; that they will listen to you, truly listen to you, they will always be there for you, always be by your side; that you are equal and work together as such and you grow together. The true meaning of trust stems from the feeling of safety; that someone trusts you because they feel safe with you; that you are dependable and won't let them down. We trust our partner to keep our heart safe and not to break it, just like a child will trust a mother to keep them safe from harm.

Establishing trust takes time in a relationship – it takes years to develop and can be destroyed in seconds. Once destroyed, it can never be fixed. Not really, not fully. It is why it is the single most important facet of a company's culture, because without trust, you are left with its dark opposite; fear.

If you are afraid of someone, you will not feel safe and you will not trust them. You will be fearful that they will hurt you; fearful that they will let you down; fearful that they are not by your side; that they are not where you need them. If you live in fear of someone, they will have control over you. They will not respect you; you will not be their equal and you will not grow together.

Fear is the greatest killer in a relationship. Once it enters, it never leaves and it spreads like wildfire. Once fear penetrates, it finds a way into every aspect of a relationship and starts eroding trust, rapidly causing destruction and breaking down resistance until all you are left with are bitter memories and sadness.

In an organisation, fear will cause the same effect and it is like a virus that grows faster as trust is eroded.

Trust and respect are also about responsibility. If you have a closely monitored team where they do not have the responsibility to make decisions, and any approvals must be made outside of the team by Management, they will always be fearful of making mistakes. You are also adding an extra layer of complexity to your processes. Teams will feel that they don't have the confidence or the appreciation from their leaders.

I recently conducted a survey of 100 CEOs on what they felt the level of trust was like in their organisation, ranging from small to large, within a widespread blend of industries.

Over 85% of CEOs felt that they had a good level of trust, with the remaining 15% or so feeling they had a high level of trust. Remarkably, none regarded there to be any fear in their organisation. Other aspects of the survey included questions on experimentation, understanding how open they are to mistakes being made, and also the level of autonomy for teams (which is a clear indicator of trust). However, what they were unaware of was that the survey was also a little behavioural experiment about them, albeit a simple one.

What I wanted to prove was that whilst we want to believe that everything is rosy in the garden, and that our people trust each other working in a no-fear environment, when you stand back and take an objective view, there is still some work to do.

My survey proved that despite responders marking down that they believed there was a high level of trust, there was no culture of experimentation where teams can feel they can make mistakes and learn. We also found that teams did not have autonomy to take responsibility for their work. Therefore, it can be concluded here that there is a desire to have trust, but in actual fact the reality is that there is very little.

In most instances, it can be argued that Senior Executives in business would prefer there wasn't a culture of fear in their organisation. No one sets out for this, just like the majority of people don't enter into a relationship with the intention of creating fear in their partner. We want there to be trust within an organisation, but just desiring it is not enough. No one will admit that there actually is a culture of fear, because either they don't believe it, or they don't see it. Either way, they have a problem, and this is where the foundations must be built, with a genuine desire to change.

In his book, 'The Five Dysfunctions of a Team', Patrick Lencioni explains how having trust is the first foundation required in the building of high-performing teams across the organisation. As a leader of an organisation, you have to build a culture of trust and respect, otherwise, your people will be too fearful to grow.

All of your employees will have something to bring to the table. Some of them may not be the most experienced or the most skilled, but they will be full of ideas and their own unique experiences. They must be given the freedom to experiment; the freedom to make decisions, collectively as a team, without the fear of failure or mistakes. They must be safe in the knowledge that if something doesn't quite work, they will not be chastised for trying.

Breaking down the Silos

We have talked at length about Agile teams being cross-functional, and breaking down silos to work together in collaboration whilst delivering continuous value and closing feedback loops.

This is absolutely essential for teams to become high-performing and successful Agile entities.

The organisation itself has a duty to break down silos even further by encouraging cross-functionality and closer collaboration throughout all teams, to enhance the value and success at the enterprise level.

Whilst as a team you may not be able to influence that at a strategic level, you can certainly do as much as you can to work closer together with other teams to bring down silos and encourage greater collaboration. Get closer to your Marketing teams, Sales teams, and Operations teams.

Invite them in as they are as much a part of your team as those working day to day. And remember, it is all about the customer. The more you understand each other's needs, the more the customer will benefit.

Think of how you may break silos down. Are you currently structured with separate Marketing, Sales, Operations, Development, Testing and Delivery entities? What can you do to bring these closer together, even working cross-functionally together? How can you bridge the gaps and even structure working environments for greater collaboration and communication flow?

BMW is an excellent example of breaking down organisational silos in their car manufacturing plant in Germany. As described in detail in his book 'Project to Product', Mik Kersten describes how each individual team is connected, and how they collaborate together right across the plant. Even more remarkable is that you are able to see the operational workflow from space.

Of course, I am not talking via acute heat maps, but through greater visual clarity because of the positioning of the building. Its end-to-end processes can be followed right across the plant from one end right through to the other.

Think of life before phones, text messaging and email (otherwise known as instant communication). Think of a life we are so familiar with that we take it for granted. We receive messages at the click of a button. If we just go back as far as the 16th century, where a poor farmer who was unable to write would have had to rely on direct oral messaging, or perhaps a scribe to interpret the message to be passed on across to a different town just for perhaps a change in requirements on a particular cattle purchase.

There was so much reliance on the correct interpretation, and delay in ensuring the message was passed on in time. if the purchase has already been made, the change in requirement could not be fulfilled. If the correct message was misinterpreted, there was a risk to the correct purchase happening. It would have meant that when making purchases, these factors would all have to be considered and possibly overcompensated for in the event of changes in circumstances, to avoid having to make changes further down the line.

400 years on, entire organisations still operate in similar ways; where silos between multiple teams cause additional complexities in communication, activity and approvals; where baton passing causes unnecessary delays and waste. Consequently, silo operations will only be effective within their own entity.

This subsequently compels a culture of single-mindedness and individualism, an 'us and them' type culture, i.e., we're okay and we don't really care about them, or even encouraging blame, i.e., it was the guys in Marketing. It was their fault because they were late giving us the requirements.

By adopting a WE mindset across the organisation, you will create togetherness and belonging in every part of the company, encouraging problem-solving across teams and all serving one customer, where everyone has a collective responsibility.

It helps that the strict, complex processes that enforce silo operations are stripped out, and, of course, that your teams are not in competition with each other. Therefore, as leaders, you must support the concept of WE by adopting different practices where healthy competition and collaborative processes are in place. These must not then be at the expense of delivering continuous value to the customer.

CHAPTER FIVE

The Agile Operation

"A bad system will beat good people every time"

W. Edwards Demming
Author and Lecturer

Start With Where You Are

Let's start by looking at a real-life example.

I once coached a Development and Operations (DevOps) team in a marketing communications function of a major telecommunications organisation in the UK. The team had just been formed by the merger of separate Development and Operations teams.

The first thing we needed to do was create the reality on their "work board". The Scrum Master asked for the whole team to add their work items to a newly formed product backlog, with a view to deciding which tasks would make up the next sprint. The Product Owner had a couple of user stories to go into the sprint but was content that the team needed to clear out some legacy work before they could start working together as a proper collaborative and cross-functional team. That was okay; it's better that a team is given the chance to tidy things up so that they can fully focus.

The objective or sprint goal, therefore, was to deliver a small number of new user stories whilst getting into a position to be fully focused on the next sprint.

The Operations board followed a fairly complex system and workflow due to the nature of the work. The Development board was far simpler, containing only three stages: To Do, In Progress and Done.

The Scrum Master and Product Owner decided it would be better to have a simple board to start off with and build out from there.

However, simplicity doesn't reflect the reality for new Agile teams (though it should certainly be the aspiration).

Starting with where you want to end up simply masks the major problem areas you need to fix in the operation, as you need to create a clear view of what's going on end-to-end and refine each step as you go.

In Agile practice, we consider processes as systems and the aim of each team is to break down its system into component parts in order to identify areas of waste to optimise for efficiency and effectiveness. We call this practice LEAN Systems Thinking.

The art of "systems thinking" is the ability to stand back from the operation and seek out areas for continuous improvement by way of focusing on each component part of a team's operational process.

If a new Agile team starts with where it hopes it will end up, (its optimal state), it will be impossible to separate what is working well and what needs changing.

The most common framework used to manage a team's system is Kanban. Originating in the early 1950s in Japan by Toyota manufacturing, it was devised as a way to visualise the operational process of the manufacturing of its vehicles with a view to optimising efficiencies. Its creator, Taiichi Ohno, designed the first Kanban visual board and operational system after recognising the inefficiencies in their production line as he sought ways to better their processes.

In creating a live visual of the operational system, each member of a team can manage their workload across the complete end-to-end workflow and look for areas to improve as a collective.

So, start with where you are today so you can get a "real-world" view and establish a working system. From there, you can look to reduce workflow steps over time to continue to optimise and improve.

Because of its versatility in focusing on workflow process, it can be adapted into any scenario, team, programme or service delivery operation from the senior leadership team of a major telecommunications company through to a busy high-street restaurant.

Being Transparent at all Levels

Showing transparency or "being transparent" is the buzz phrase of the decade. I hear it everywhere I go. It's almost as if it is programmed into leaders as part of the 'What Makes a Good Leader' manual.

But it's one of the hardest things to get right. It isn't just an activity; nor is it solely a behavioural trait. It's deeper than that. It's cultural, just like trust.

And there is nothing like showing complete transparency to help build trust in your people.

But it's a two-way street. We give teams all the tools they need to help them manage their workload and demonstrate progress of the work that they do, showing their own transparency. But unfortunately, it doesn't always come back the other way.

Being transparent is only possible when, as a leader, you are able to show your vulnerability; for it is what you expose that helps to provide the clarity necessary to appreciate where everyone stands.

A position of vulnerability provides the platform for accountability. Being accountable – as in, showing integrity and responsibility for your decisions and actions – is the sign of true leadership. Forget all the buzzwords.

We'll look a little closer at the role of an Agile Leader later in this book but here is some guidance on how Agile organisations embed a culture of transparency.

1. **Leadership Kanban board:** provide clear visibility and management of your own workload in terms of strategic direction, high-level issues to solve and a clear golden thread from the highest objectives in the organisation through to the teams on the ground.
2. **Easy access:** avoid stringent security processes in order to enable interested parties to come and see progress.
3. **Live data feed:** for real-time progress and status of products and services, with a focus on how you can help your people to drive efficiencies and effectiveness in Agile practice.

4. **Clear and managed escalation path:** set up a system for issues which cannot be resolved within the team, and therefore need to be escalated. You will see an example of an escalation system which I helped leaders implement below.

5. **Simplicity is key:** create clear visibility with little effort and complexity to help understand what is going on (and where) at all levels of the organisation.

It is time to move away from progress status reports. These take time to prepare and are usually out of date by the time they are sent; they also take time away from you as leaders focusing on the bigger picture. Instead, set up visible boards with live data to provide a real-time snapshot.

Create a culture of visibility and transparency at all levels to be in a position to see whatever is going on at any one point without the need to receive regular reports. There is a term in Japanese called "Gemba", which means "walk the wall". Take time out of your day/week to go and walk the wall with your teams to understand how they are getting on and where they may need your support.

Create an Escalation System

Saab Aeronautics used Agile practices to build and produce the new multi-role strike fighter, the JAS 39E Saab Gripen.

Each morning at 7.30 am, the Engineers on the ground gathered in their respective squads for a Daily Scrum (15 minutes) to align on the work in progress and raise any issues to be escalated to the next level. At 7.45 am, the first layer of Management came together for a Scrum of Scrums with the Scrum Master of each squad, to discuss escalated issues and solve problems. Any issues that could not be resolved went up the chain for the next layer Scrum of Scrums at 8.00 am and so on. By 8.45, the highest Executives were fully aligned to the work and in the right position to completely clear the blockers to progress for the Engineers on the ground. It took just 1 hour and 15 minutes every day for problems to be solved; an efficient, effective system for issue resolution and alignment.

If it can happen in the military, with pre-historic process and bureaucracy, it can literally happen anywhere. You just need the right structure and willingness to buy into this mindset.

In Agile, we refine the level of communication by eliminating the need for progress update meetings that can drag on for hours and which take considerable time for preparation beforehand with de-briefing afterwards.

Using clear, visible boards to aid discussions and manage issues, each team can provide updates and discuss escalations in real-time. With proper transparency, this can happen all the way up the chain of command.

Escalations should be considered as the type of issues that cannot be solved by the individual team and therefore require support from Management.

They can be broken down into 4 categories:

People: ensure the right skills and capability for the team to deliver the right value continuously.

Process: help support changes in processes to ensure continuous value, delivery, and rapid response capability for your teams.

Technology: work tirelessly to ensure the very best technology is in place to provide the capability necessary for your teams to deliver continuous value to your customers.

Structure: set up for success by structuring teams to get as close to your customers as possible without the need for handoffs to 3rd parties and management approvals.

Set the boundaries of responsibility for your teams as wide as possible, enabling them to make key decisions. Consequently, you can focus on the bigger picture at a more strategic level. Be visible and available in order to support issues that block the progress of the team. Review regularly, ensuring that you are not the bottleneck for progress.

Here are some examples of real and typical escalated issues with priority levels, that cannot be solved at a team level. Which ones can you empower the teams to fix?

Scrum of Scrums Priority Examples

Priority	Priority Definition	Category Label	Examples
High	A critical impediment with very high impact User Story/Team blocked	Technology	Development Environment is down and therefore unavailable
		Process	Release process is not available which is blocking progress
		People	The lead developer is leaving the company at the end of the sprint
		Structure	There is a 3rd-party dependency on a current user story which is blocking progress
Medium	A major impediment with significant impact User Story/Team able to progress, but quality may be lower	Technology	Development Environment is extremely slow, causing serious delays
		Process	Release process is currently outside of the team causing major delays
		People	The lead developer has been signed off sick for the rest of the sprint
		Structure	There is a 3rd-party dependency on a user story for an up-and-coming sprint which will cause major delays in progress
Low	User Story/Team able to progress, low impact on quality	Technology	Development Environment is slow, causing some delays
		Process	Release process is inside the team but is manual which is causing minor delays
		People	There is a user story that requires certain skills training to fulfil
		Structure	There is a 3rd-party dependency on a future user story which may cause minor delays in progress

It is the System, not the People.

Earlier in the book, we talked about how Agile organisations move away from having a culture of blame to deflect accountability and avoid solving deep-rooted problems. Instead, they look at the general system of the operation. We are all products of the environment we work in, the tools we are given to do the work and the processes by which we are governed to deliver value.

The purpose is to assure that the team hone in on their operational system rather than the shortcomings of each other, to remove the need to blame and rather focus on improving how they work in order to drive towards becoming a high-performing entity.

Having regular "retrospectives" will give everyone the chance to improve the team's system. By looking at specific areas such as skills, process, tools and technology, you make sure that such improvements are carried out as part of the day-to-day practice. And of course, if these types of issues cannot be solved at team level, then there is a system for escalation.

Using key data from the ways of working will give team members the chance to optimise and also enhance their system.

Teams must be given the airspace and time to improve how they work together. If they are under continuous pressure to deliver and are constantly being changed around, moved into other teams and having a high attrition rate, their chances of becoming high-performing will diminish considerably.

Back when I was a humble Scrum Master at a software company, our Retrospectives were a ceremonial event. In the early days, they had little impact on improvements being made, simply because we did not have ownership, accountability, or a solid escalation procedure. Eventually, one of my lead developers approached me to state that the Retrospectives were becoming more and more pointless because nothing ever changed.

For the following Retrospective, I was determined to change the outcome. I suggested that we take just two improvements into the next sprint, but for each improvement, I needed ownership, and that the owner would be accountable for the delivery. However, I assured them I would support them to ensure a successful outcome. What I needed was for the Product Owner to agree that they would be prioritised in the sprint, therefore reducing the scope of new work. In actual fact, what we needed to do was create a rule of thumb that only a certain percentage of new work could be taken into the sprint, and a small percentage for improvement, ensuring that we could allocate sufficient time.

This was not an easy conversation to be had, but I convinced the PO that it should be seen as an investment and that we would see the benefits later on.

And so it happened that for that specific sprint, we delivered on our commitment and the team became much more motivated to participate in the ceremony of the Retrospective.

At the next Retro, we decided to create a policy of new work making up 90% of the team's effort with the remaining 10% dedicated to improving our ways of working. This eventually changed to 80/20% which then included a greater drive towards clearing out technical debt* which had built up in the background and was starting to cause some real pain, not to mention an increase in the level of defects coming back to us from our live production system.

---

* In software, technical debt is a term used to describe functionality that requires rework, has become obsolete or out of date and will eventually cause problems in the system. If not kept in control, it can ultimately lead to considerable work and costs. Agile teams tend to have a policy of making sure any technical debt is given ongoing attention.

In this scenario, the team moved away from the mindset of blame, that nothing ever changes, where we were simply going through the motions, to a more productive and systems-based mindset. We focused on creating a principle to ensure improvements were made continuously with a clear focus on the system and ways of working of the team incorporating strong accountability for everyone.

Now, here's a challenge for you as a leader. When was the last time you took a step back and really looked at the system you are working within? When was the last time you brought your leadership team into the room to identify areas to improve in each of the four categories? Get into the habit of doing this regularly, making allowances (even policy) for each of your teams to do the same.

Using Visual Tools to Manage Your Operation

There are a multitude of tools available to help teams and management to run and create strong visibility of their operation. One of the original Agile principles was that in order to build successful, high-performing teams, they should be co-located. The original visual tool back in 2001 would have been a physical board to provide visibility of a team's

Scrum or Kanban operation. A co-located team would have centred around the board on a daily basis to align on the work and to raise and escalate issues. The Scrum Master would manually calculate the data to understand team capability and identify areas for improvement. The tangible action of moving tickets along a physical board, showing live completion of the work provided each member with a sense of satisfaction and achievement.

Nowadays, and with the evolution of broadband capability, flexible working, shared offices and remote working, the concept of co-located teams has had to evolve in itself. No longer are we restricted by the need to be physically present in the same place in order to create and deliver continuous value as a collaborative, cross-functional unit. In fact, I've coached Agile teams spread across 4 different time zones, with different cultures and ways of working, who have developed into high-performing entities. But that was only possible in a relentless commitment and desire for every member to build relations and find ways for team members to collaborate together regularly, even on occasion to come together physically, where possible. But the main focus was not on the tools being used, but in how they interacted.

The original Agile value of **People and interactions over Processes and Tools** should not be underestimated.

The types of tools we use should only support and supplement a team's collaboration and management of the work and not vice versa, i.e., shoe-horning a team around a specific tool or process. So, the tool used to manage the work should not dictate how the team works.

What are we trying to achieve? The main use of having a visible board is to help the team manage the work, to prioritise and also to establish the right system in order to continuously improve. For Agile leaders, it is to understand how the team are getting on and where they may need your support. For everyone, it is to create transparency and a real-time view of the situation and progress being made, with sufficient detail to drill down into.

Some common principles to help guide you on visible tools:

1. Simplicity. Try not to over-engineer.
2. Try to simulate the team being in the same room as best as possible – use interactive screens and other technologies available to support.
3. Integrate systems with different value streams and management.

4. Allow responsibility for teams to configure and continuously improve their system without disrupting the integrity of the platform.
5. Set up visual aids to provide live data to reduce the need to produce status reports.

Therefore, find the best tool to suit the structure and requirements of the organisation. Find a tool with versatility that is seamlessly configurable and easily scalable.

Australian provider Atlassian are perhaps the most common and comprehensive of suppliers to manage Agile operations. Founded in 2002 by Mike Cannon-Brookes and Scott Farquhar, their flagship product Jira was originally created as an engineering tool to manage bug resolutions. Within a few years, Jira evolved into what we now know as a platform for managing Scrum and Kanban operation systems.

Its sister tool, Confluence, was created in 2004 as a collaboration tool (or more commonly *wiki*), to help manage documents, policies and general information for value streams.

Both tools integrate with a multitude of plug-ins to enhance the operation of both, but remember rule number one: keep it simple – especially at the beginning.

And utilise both applications for their main purpose: Jira to help manage and visualise the system and the work (value), and Confluence to help manage and visualise the information.

Typically, Agile organisations will restrict systems administration to a select few, whilst providing configuration rights by value stream. You may want to consider having a community of practice, just as with Agile roles and ways of working, but specifically for the chosen tool. A Jira community will help ensure consistency and best practice and also establish a set-up that works across the organisation.

To conclude this part – I absolutely love and will always have a preference for physical boards – there is nothing like clear and live information available in full view, with the satisfaction of moving your work through to completion for everyone to see, but most importantly, for support where required. There is a term that highlights the difference between physical and electronic boards; Information Radiators (Physical Boards) and Information Fridges (Electronic Tool). An Information Radiator radiates heat, providing a real-time indication of the situation. An Information Fridge requires the need to open it up in order to access a view of the team's board. So, if you do have to use an electronic solution, be mindful of the need to show live information in full view to highlight when you may need to support teams in real-time, as well as having easy access to understanding progress.

Using the Data to Help Improve Your System and Become Predictable

Once you have a suitable visual tool in place and your teams are starting to manage their workload, the use of data will become vital in enabling continuous improvement towards becoming high-performing.

And the data can reveal a whole host of hidden secrets; from team velocity, to assisting with future planning and the level of delay caused by impediments.

One thing I am always conscious of in using data to gauge performance is that it can do harm: it can be used as a stick with which to beat the team. For example, using User Story Points as a metric of success or failure in sprints.

In the example below, in Sprint 5 the team delivered 40 story points, Sprint 6 – 32 points and Sprint 7 – 40 points – bringing the average down to 37.3 points. Instead of chastising the team for under-delivering, I would instead look a little closer.

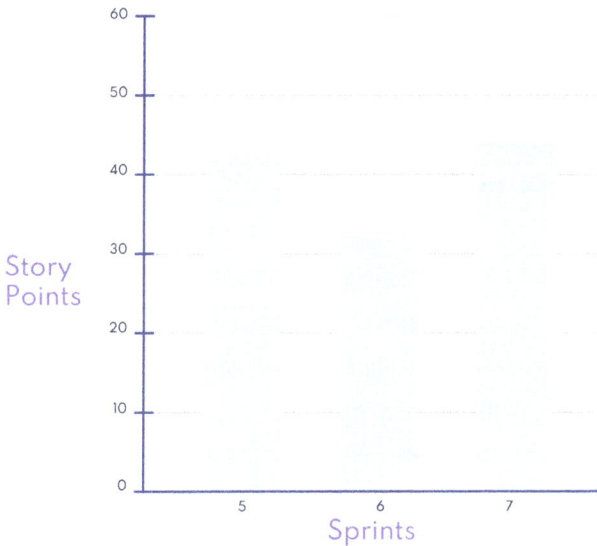

Fig 5.1: Example of story points delivered per sprint for trend analysis

I'd look at Sprint 6 and establish whether perhaps someone was on holiday or on sick leave. Or perhaps there was an impediment that caused unforeseen delays. Or maybe there was a User Story that was underestimated and when the team got into it, it was larger than they initially thought. Maybe they just couldn't finish it because they didn't have the right permissions. There is always a reason. But looking at the data through the lens of continuous improvement as opposed to blame, will mean that going forward, we can support them and help them to become more predictable.

Evaluate whether they need additional training on estimating their work. Is there a problem with sickness? Are they being pushed too hard and burning out? Is the impediment an anomaly or does it come up regularly? Can we look at removing it permanently? Is this approval step necessary? Can we give the team additional responsibility?

The data can therefore be a powerful indicator where support may be required. And it is part of the role of the Scrum Master to keep track of what the data is telling us in calculating trends through averages.

The role is critical to ensure teams can become high-performing. Whilst it is not an analyst role, it does require basic, analytical skills in order to identify where the team may require support and improvement.

Each step in the process, as well as each element of the team's structure and ways of working, should be broken down into components in order to identify areas that can be improved, and the data is key to supporting this.

As your Agile teams settle into a sustained pace and begin to become predictable, your Product Owners will then be able to use data in order to forward plan and consequently have greater confidence that delivery promises can be met.

One note of caution to be made, and it is something that Agile Coaches see in so many of the organisations that we work with: Sustainability and predictability go hand in hand; they are not mutually exclusive. You cannot have predictable teams without them being settled and sustainable. You will need to help them as best you can to settle down and reduce the need to move members in and out of teams ensuring that each member is dedicated and focused. At the same time, support the Scrum Masters to work with the data to help their teams improve as required.

Only then will your teams become predictable.

CHAPTER SIX

Becoming a Value Centric Organisation

> *"Don't find customers for your products.
> Find products for your customers."*
> Seth Godin
> Author

What Does Value Mean to Your Customers?

In my time working in Agile practice, I have come to realise (and it has taken a while), that primarily, Agile organisations are value-centric, meaning that they focus all their efforts on providing continuous value to their customers. I mentioned earlier in the book that Blockbuster's final days were aimed at extracting as much profit from its customers as possible. They had misjudged their customers' needs and focused too much on pleasing shareholders rather than identifying exactly what value they were providing to their customers. Consequently, they paid the ultimate price.

Value can come in all different shapes and sizes depending on your customers' needs. To a busy businesswoman using a mobile phone, value could be the ease of use and navigation around the device in order to communicate at speed.

To an elderly gentleman who has poor eyesight, it could be the simplicity and accessibility functions of his device. For a removals company, value for the customer would be the care taken in the transportation of their goods. And more often than not, we would be happier to pay slightly more in order to have peace of mind. As the saying goes, you do tend to get what you pay for.

Price is the one facet we associate with value. Don't we just love a bargain? A 2 for the price of 1 offer is seen as great value. We identify the benefit immediately of having paid half the price for double the value. But we become very suspicious when we see a low price or offer that seems a bit too good to be true. Usually, it's because it is, and our instincts and experience act as good warning signs.

Being value-centric doesn't just help focus on the customer's needs but puts every effort and priority into responding to those needs as fast as possible, thereby making sure that the customer is the priority and is being served way ahead of your competitors.

Close the Feedback Loop Tight

The distance between your customers and your teams in today's world is one of the key measurables in how Agile you are as an organisation.

But just getting close to your customers is not going to make you Agile on its own. How responsive you are to feedback (meaning the pace at which you can respond) is what will enable real business agility.

Being responsive is going to set you apart. Understanding your customer's needs, forecasting where those needs may change and being able to adapt and respond at pace are imperative.

Unfortunately, in many of the organisations I work with, I often see that this is the area that is missed the most; either misinterpreted or half measured.

Becoming an Agile organisation isn't just sending your staff on a training course and expecting that now they can go faster and do more. "We are now Agile," they say whilst maintaining the same processes and steps, team structures, leadership styles, management layers and general risk-averse culture.

So let me be absolutely clear on what is involved here: Tightening your feedback loop so tight that you almost have your customer in the room (and, in some cases, that could be possible), takes willingness, courage and, most of all, acceptance that things need to change now. Such acceptance, willingness and courage come from the very top and cascades down.

This means **restructuring teams** to create the shortest route to your customer and ensuring a **feedback loop** to continuously deliver value, understand changes in need and be fully responsive.

This also means **delegating responsibility** to your teams to make decisions that could directly impact or hinder delivering continuous value to your customers.

This means giving teams the **freedom to innovate** and experiment with ideas that may or may not solve your customers' problems – getting feedback, learning, measuring success and adapting.

All the big Agile organisations follow this way of working – Amazon are structured to make up to 1000 software releases per day. In ONE day! Some companies don't even have the capability to make this many releases in ten years! Amazon's Development Teams are structured with fully cross-functional teams. They put all the responsibility and decision-making as close to their customers as possible, and are continuously innovating.

If something isn't quite working for the customer, they have the capability to fix it and release it even before the customer even knows it's happened.

Their feedback loop is tight, they have streamlined processes to enable responsiveness, and they have fully autonomous teams to manoeuvre at this pace.

Fear of Failure

So why do non-Agile organisations not recognise this as the key to success in modern business? It is because of a fear of failure, plain and simple. Organisations put so much effort into avoiding making mistakes through complex processes and additional resources. Some large organisations will have Change Management Boards; a whole group of people tasked with reviewing and managing change. I've seen six months of work going to a Change Board and being rejected on the basis of risk. How much money has been lost? How much delay has been caused?

"But what happens if someone makes a mistake? We can't afford to make mistakes," they remonstrate.

HM Revenue & Customs (HMRC) is one of the largest employers in the UK. It is the Government department responsible for the administration and collection of all UK taxes.

Their structures and processes have been designed to protect the integrity of the data and complex operation involved in administration and collection of taxes, and therefore risk management is of the highest importance. As a result, things manoeuvre at a very, very slow pace, causing additional challenges, especially when the requirement for change is needed.

There is an engrained culture of a fear of failure. In 2007, 25 million records went missing when a disc containing data of the tax records of UK families was sent through the normal post, rather than a secure and safe courier. The lost disc was not even reported for 3 weeks, causing even greater risk to fraudulent behaviour on a nationwide scale. A huge embarrassment for the Government.

This would never happen again.

The chief of HMRC, Sir Paul Gray resigned.

The Chancellor of the Exchequer, Alistair Darling said at the time that it was an "extremely serious failure on the part of HMRC to protect sensitive personal data entrusted to it in breach of its own guidelines" and blamed mistakes made by junior officials. A HMRC spokeswoman said. "The junior HMRC official involved should have notified their senior officials but did not."

In an independent review of the incident, it was found that HMRC was considered "woefully inadequate" in its handling of sensitive data.

How could it be possible for such a breach in security and integrity to happen? Could it have been possible that the junior officials involved were so fearful of retribution that they tried to cover up the mistake and realised eventually that they just had to come clean?

With fairly good reason, though to its detriment, HMRC added huge layers of complexity in its processes to avoid such an error ever happening again. The time and effort involved today in accessing and processing data, and making improvements to its digital systems is so extreme that by the time a new feature goes live it is so out of date that the technical debt built up in creating new tech on more advanced systems, means that it would cost double to fix it.

When I was coaching teams there, they had a process for dealing with what they called HPIs. These are High Priority Incidents. Basically, if a bug in the system brought the system down, it would be considered a HPI. The lead engineer of the platform where the bug was found would be on the call. The project manager of the project where the lead engineer was being called away from would be on the call. 1-2 testers who would be involved in the fix would be on the call. A few stakeholders who had a direct link to the incident would be on the call. And about 30 others; from senior managers, technical architects, test managers, business analysts, senior engineers and data scientists would also be on the call. Usually lead by the production or live support manager. For no particular reason I would be asked to join the call occasionally as I was working closely with some of the data teams.

I had absolutely no input whatsoever.

The call would be a chance for the lead engineer to provide an update on what was happening with the bug fix, what investigation was happening, what the team are currently trying and what to expect next. It was also a chance for technical people to talk technical about whichever would be the best route forward.

A HPI call would take place every hour on the hour and would take approximately 15-20 minutes. Sometimes even longer. Every hour, even overnight!

I always felt sorry for the lead engineer. What pressure to be under, and not really having much chance to progress. But most of all, the fear of failure he must have had each and every hour that went past until eventually a fix could be achieved, tested, deployed and normal service resuming.

So as mentioned in The Agile Culture chapter. Building trust is essential. Being clear in the messaging is key as a leader that you have their back, to provide the environment for teams to be responsive, that you are not a bottleneck, equally that you do not have strict change processes in place to avoid risk. If they want to try something that is going to help us learn something about the customer, then go for it. After all, what's the worst that can happen?

Using Behavioural Data to Learn About Your Customers

I don't know about you, but I get hit with requests for feedback pretty much on a daily basis. *Score your experience out of 5; Share your experience; please write a comment about the product you have recently purchased; tell us how we can improve.*

All useful data points. Understanding how your customers feel about your products and services will no doubt provide you with much better improvement opportunities.

For example, getting a ride in an Uber will always finish with a request for feedback on the driver. Well, here's the thing. If you do not give a score of 5, the driver will be penalised and will lose customers as a result. Uber are creating competition between drivers. That is surely wrong, isn't it? I never give top marks in the feedback I give. I always believe there is room for improvement. But what are their internal expectations based on? The perfect experience? This got me thinking. What are the criteria that I need to base my feedback on? Is it:

- promptness and punctuality of both the driver arriving and me getting to my destination?
- pristinely kept car?
- polished and well-groomed driver?
- communicative (or at least appreciative of whether a conversation is sought) and keeping it in safe conversational territory, i.e., no religion or politics?
- safe driving? (I've been with a few Lewis Hamilton wannabees!)

How can all of these score top marks, ever?

I then realised that I am also given a rating as a customer. I am 4.83 at the last reading. So not top marks, but I wonder what I am being scored on. Will it be higher if I were to give top marks to my driver?

I wondered just how misrepresented the scoring system really was, and I just ended up with the same question.

Why?

What's the point of feedback? What purpose does it serve whether I score my driver a 4 or a 5, other than to ensure that they will not be penalised as a result? And my experience isn't just with the driver. They represent Uber in all respects, from the use of the app all the way through to me arriving safely at my destination.

Should I, therefore, rate the driver based on whether the app was "glitchy" or running slowly, or if there was a system error?

How does the driver know that the service provided has served its purpose to the satisfaction of the customer? How do Uber know?

The scoring system does nothing more than create animosity amongst the drivers; it does absolutely nothing to help improve the customer experience.

Staying on the subject of taxi drivers:

There is a yellow cab driver in New York whose mission it is to provide the best experience he can to his customers; as if they are in a limousine. It is even written on the business card he passes to his passengers as they enter his cab.

From the sheer spotlessness and cleanliness of the vehicle, to the complimentary bottle of water on ice and the choice of complimentary newspapers, sweets and general considerations he takes into account with questions like, "Are you in a hurry or would you like me to go at the speed limit?" are all part of the service he provides.

He asks for a business card from his clients at the end of the journey, and always writes a thank you email after the journey.

His focus is on providing the most value that he can to his passengers. His main differentiator is this. He will always ask his passengers, "Is there anything you felt could have been improved upon on your journey today?" He wants to keep his feedback loop tight. This particular taxicab never has to sit and wait in the rank for customers; they always come to him.

He doesn't have a scoring system, but simply understands his customers' needs and ensures he is responsive to change.

But let's go back to the Uber rating system. Let's say from now on, knowing what we know about the penalty for not getting a score of 5 every time, that everyone, all Uber customers, rate the drivers a 5, regardless of whether it is deserved or not. What then happens to Uber? Do they sit back and look at it and think, "Wow! We have some of the best taxi drivers in the world"? How do they then penalise their drivers?

Fundamentally, what we have here is simply that we are rating a service based on our opinion, i.e., how we feel as individuals, what our experience has been and maybe even the effect it has had on our mood, be that good or bad.

But this does absolutely nothing to ensure that Uber as an organisation could ever improve. In fact, all that feedback does is provide the company with a way to punish its drivers. Now, some may argue that maybe Uber are aiming to rate their drivers to help nurture excellence; i.e., if the drivers are actually providing an excellent service, then their rating should be a five, and this, in turn, acts as a form of incentive.

This line of thinking IS fair. But what if, for some reason, I am in a particularly bad mood that day. I simply got out of bed on the wrong side, it's a bad hair day and nothing has gone right for me all day. I then get into an Uber and don't even notice the complimentary water. I just don't even focus on the drive at all. I just want to get home. I then give a random 4-star rating, not even caring why.

What will this suggest to Uber? That their driver needs to improve. I hadn't noticed him give the most relaxed and enjoyable drive. He even took the scenic route for my own pleasure. There was only one thing to complain about and it wasn't even the driver. There was a delay in the app when I had booked my ride; nothing major, but it may have indirectly contributed to my mood and, subsequently, influenced my overall rating. It hadn't occurred to me that the driver would be penalised, and guess what…this is probably what happened.

So, while we believe that our opinion matters, it can certainly cloud the overall analysis of feedback. What we actually need to understand are the behaviours of our customers and to really, genuinely learn how our products and services are helping or hindering.

Behavioural data analysis is now as fundamental to the success of an organisation as the top sales person in the company. Large Agile organisations are spending serious money on making sure that they are way ahead of the game.

The way your customers use your products and services, and whether they are helping or hindering them, can provide you with such valuable information.

Also, knowing how your customers are using your products and services is as important as why they may not be using them.

Going back to the Blockbuster example: Behavioural data analysis would have saved them from extinction. They would have had enough data to challenge what was going on and been able to better predict how people's needs were changing, rather than focusing all their efforts on increasing profit capability.

With Uber, using behavioural data analysis could help them to understand the needs of their customers better (just like the New York cabbie, but at scale), which could ensure the sustainability of the company, rather than focusing on internal competition amongst their drivers.

Therefore, organisations will need to do exactly this in order to not only survive, but thrive in the modern world. Knowing how your customers are using your products and services is imperative, but not in an opinion-based way. We know opinions* can't be controlled, but we can control how our products and services are being used and whether they are solving our customers' problems.

---

*   *Opinions can, of course, change, and we can have some influence on that. However, in order to be one step ahead, we need to use opinions to help improve services and subsequently use this behaviour to drive the transformation of the company.*

User Acceptance Testing

Imagine a world where your customers are working so closely with your Development Teams that you can establish a really tight feedback loop; a loop that will ensure and sustain the success of your products and services.

Imagine a world where the concept of feedback is built entirely on the way that you work; that it becomes standard practice and just a given.

Imagine a world where you are so in tune with your customer needs that you are able to make important decisions early, and respond as needs change.

Agile organisations incorporate and continuously encourage feedback and acceptance from their users on an ongoing basis.

Working closely with the team, even being part of the team, and providing opinion and behaviour feedback continuously, provides real-time understanding of the strength and usability of its products and services.

This level of interaction should not be underestimated or feared in any way. The big challenge, however, is how to ensure you can incentivise your customers enough to play such a pivotal role, which does require a certain level of impartiality.

User Acceptance Testing starts right back at the requirements stage, where problems can be understood, and the right solution evolves.

Some organisations have focus groups that get together regularly. Ideally, you want your users to be available throughout the developmental process. Once every couple of weeks can be so effective to help test "in the wild", with just enough control and time to gather the feedback and make the relevant changes.

Controlling Change in Requirements to Ensure Sustainability

Rumour has it that if you are Agile then you should be welcoming change constantly; you must be continuously adapting.

But, allowing for continuous change will create pressure on your teams, cause hidden problems with stakeholders (where expectations become unrealistic), and consequently, teams may suffer burnout caused by excessive demand. In Agile practises, we encourage a more controlled approach to change, where negotiation is used to ensure sustainability without putting an extra burden on teams.

Let's say, for example, that the customer has a require-ment for more features. I always like to use the Agile triangle for this.

The Agile Triangle

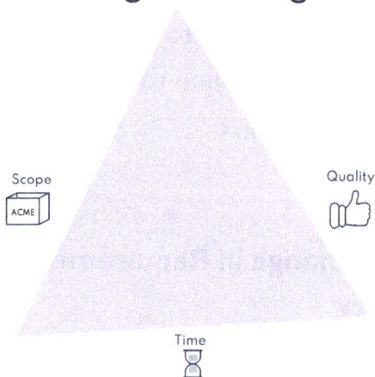

Fig 6.1: The Agile Triangle

It is a regular occurrence when I work with new teams that they are expected to maintain the same amount of **Quality** even though the **Scope** has increased and the **Time** remains the same. However, the reality is that teams cannot sustain quality under these conditions. Something has to give.

The way that Scrum can work with using 2-week iteration "sprints" is that we give the Product Owner and Scrum Master the responsibility to lock down Scope with a disciplined approach, where high-priority requirements can be worked on with dedicated focus.

The team can agree on what they will commit to in the sprint, and the Scope is set for the following two weeks. Over time, the level of Scope may increase based on the team's capability increasing as they become more settled as they work towards increasing their performance.

On occasion, there may be a need to consider something urgent that needs to be actioned immediately. Well, that is okay. Allowances are made for change/shifting priorities and urgent items. However, the Product Owner must be given the authority to negotiate, and this will be one of the biggest tests; to see that everyone in the organisation is on board; i.e. "We can absolutely take on this higher priority item, so long as it is ready to start work on.** But it will be at the expense of a lower priority item in the Sprint".

** Agile teams will have a policy to restrict work they will start work on where there is ambiguity, it does not have clear value and may be too big. This increases the opportunity for value to be delivered without delay which can be caused by requirements not having the necessary due diligence given prior to starting the work.

What will happen if this line of approach is not taken? Well, teams will simply either burn out or not deliver everything in the Sprint as they had committed to, and will, most likely, be made culpable.

What I see time and again is this sort of behaviour creeping in, and, over time, the same default response of, "Well, this Agile process isn't really working for us," or,

"We don't work in this way"

"We're not a typical Agile team"

"I know it's not the purist way, but..."

What this says to me is that there is either a level of accepted transgression, or that the teams have very little autonomy, and their stakeholders are not really on board with this new way of working.

I hear these comments a lot with new Agile teams and I challenge Senior leaders to become transparent on the level of authority they give to their teams in controlling the level of change during a Sprint cycle, and in managing their stakeholders.

Agile organisations use disciplined techniques for change and everyone respects and honours a team's policy for scope negotiations.

Managing expectations is one thing, but if you have a demanding customer you have to be in a strong position to negotiate.

With the ability to negotiate, you are reducing the risk of project failure or missed deadlines, because your teams can become much more predictable, more sustainable and more importantly, far more agile!

Value Streams – Providing Continuous Flow of Value

As I mentioned at the start of this book, the world is moving so fast and companies really need to be agile enough to adapt to continuous change in market conditions, evolving needs and generally responding far quicker than ever before by understanding their customers' needs like never before.

But also, the way we work has changed considerably over the past 20 years or so since the advent of Agile practices. Technology has helped us work more effectively and efficiently as well.

One of the greatest changes I have seen in the past few years is the movement away from traditional project management towards the advent of product and service value streams where there is no project; instead, there are end-to-end teams serving their customers with a continuous flow of value through its lifecycle. There is no project start and finish, with milestones and overspend and every 6 months going cap in hand to accounts to get more money, but a team of cross-functional skills able to design – build – test and deliver new functionality and support a product or service continuously.

Now, this may seem like a simple change, but it is major. We are already starting to see HR and Finance becoming part of programme teams with a very slow phasing out of project managers resulting in a change in the way that teams and products are budgeted for, and skills are sourced and grown. It may even go beyond this to where marketing and sales become part of the team, giving a full end-to-end stream, serving the customer needs and closing the feedback loop even more.

One of the most important facets of a successful Agile organisation is that its teams are fully cross-functional. There is no Design Team, no separate Delivery Team, Operations, Marketing etc. There are only Product Value Streams or Service Value Streams.

This isn't to say that projects will be gone forever. There will always be special initiatives and one-offs that require certain skills to come together for a small amount of time, like in construction for example, or a migration of one tool to another. But in general, product and service value streams should be strongly considered as part of an Agile re-structure.

The diagram on the next page shows the importance of having clear pathways for ideas and initiatives to be implemented and to reach the customer to enable fast feedback. The structure of the portfolio of products and suite of services enables ideas to be generated and gathered into requirements; in most cases (where possible) to be working directly with the customer to establish purpose and problems to solve, taking them through development and delivery and closing the feedback loop.

Each value stream will contain various disciplines. It is vital to bring each discipline together regularly to ensure best practice and consistency, raising and solving common issues across each value stream.

We break down silos, we bring autonomy and responsibility into each stream, and we remove excessive delays and waste caused by handoffs and approvals.

One of the major pitfalls of traditional project-focused organisations is that teams are never together for more than a few months at a time and are therefore continuously

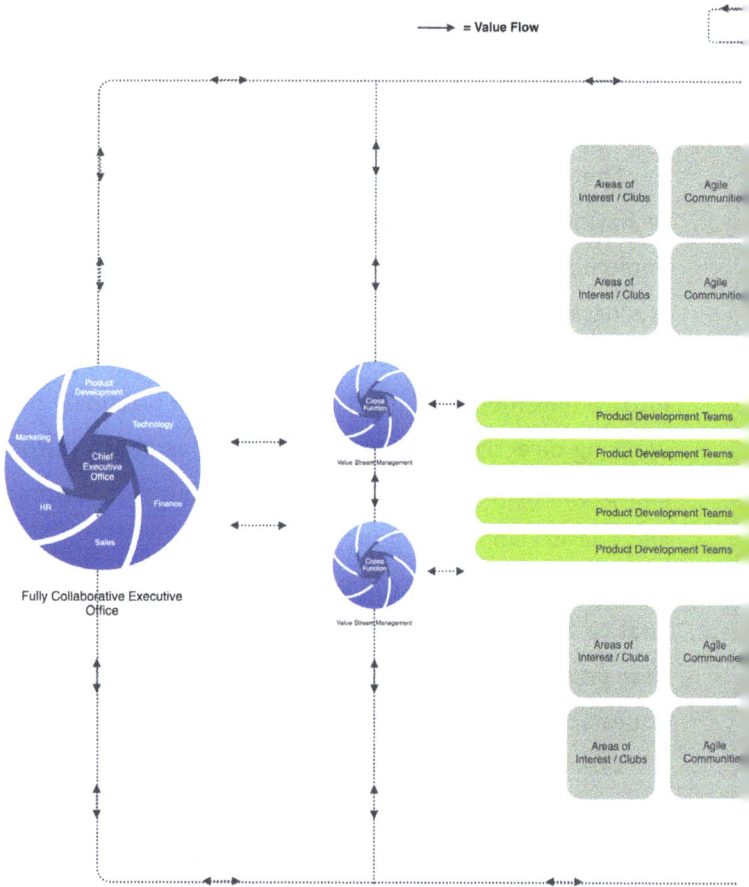

= Value Flow

Product
Development

Technology

Marketing

Chief
Executive
Office

HR

Finance

Sales

Fully Collaborative Executive
Office

Cross
Function

Value Stream Management

Cross
Function

Value Stream Management

Areas of
Interest / Clubs

Agile
Communities

Areas of
Interest / Clubs

Agile
Communities

Product Development Teams

Product Development Teams

Product Development Teams

Product Development Teams

Areas of
Interest / Clubs

Agile
Communities

Areas of
Interest / Clubs

Agile
Communities

126

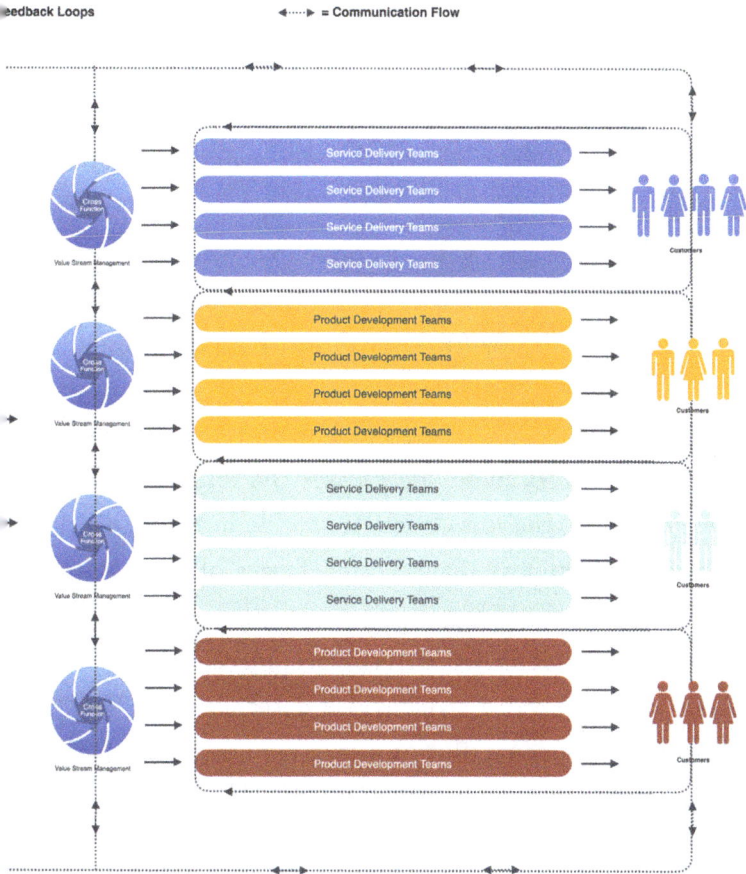

Fig 6.2: Agilistic Value Stream Scaling Framework ™

rotating, rarely settling, and working towards a state of high performance. The best of the best is then continuously "cherry-picked" and placed into one-off projects to ensure their success – without appreciating the chaos that this continuous change can cause.

Value Stream Management provides a way for teams to settle, focus, build capability and work closely with customers, ensuring a tight and continuous feedback loop and enabling the organisation as a whole to become value-centric – continuously focused on customer needs and solving problems. Everything you do as an organisation must be centred around the value that you provide to your customers.... everything! The greater the distance from your customers, the less Agile you will be in responding to change and the less chance you will have of being able to compete.

How you shape and structure your product portfolio and service suite value streams will determine just how Agile you can become. But as a rule of thumb, start off compact and keep it simple. Map out existing processes and identify areas where there will be handoffs (dependencies) and approvals. Establish technology areas that may need modernising. Where are the manual processes that can be automated, and where are there unnecessary management layers that could be slowing you down?

I would also recommend choosing a sophisticated and consistent organisation-wide tool to manage your workload across all of your value streams, where the work can become fully visual so that you can reduce the need for excessive and outdated reporting. A tool such as Jira can be so effective in supporting teams, providing visibility for management, and also highlighting areas for improvement.

But where does this leave Project Managers and middle Management? Well, they still have a place in this new world, if they are willing and have the right mindset and attitude to become a part of the transformation. A more natural fit for Project Managers would be to become Scrum Masters. But the soft skills are key as mentioned earlier in the book. Middle Managers and Line Managers can become Servant Leaders. They can step back from the day-to-day operation and look to support their people, whilst taking a broader view beyond the horizon to help with the longer-term strategy of the organisation as a whole and take a place supporting the value stream.

We'll look at funding and financing of Value Streams as opposed to more traditional project funding later in the book.

Lean Agile Funding

It is not going to be possible to transform the organisation towards optimum Business Agility without overhauling the way initiatives and projects are funded.

It is more than likely that the way initiatives and projects are budgeted is what will control prioritisation and drive the business outcomes. But in the new world of Agility, with the need to be fully responsive and adaptable to change, organisations need a more flexible and frictionless budgeting system that complements and aligns to value streams and customer demand, even going so far as to suggest integrating financial decision-making into the value stream.

Historically, budgeting of initiatives and projects is based on requirements and design, contributing to a plan that is generally out of date by the time it has even started, let alone delivered. Project Teams are directed to deliver against approved dates and targets in spite of this and possibly at the risk that the project is no longer valid. There is a tipping point on spending where the risk of wasting money already spent outweighs the realisation that the project has either failed or is no longer fit for purpose. If two out of every three projects fail, or go over budget, then this is an awful lot of waste in the business.

Modern Agile funding is centred around the value stream, where the work is brought to the teams. Value Stream Management will control the spend, aligning to rapid response and agile initiatives including innovation and ensuring continuous flow of value to the customer.

In giving control to the Value Stream, Agile teams are therefore given freedom to experiment and respond to market needs without friction or delay.

Lead Agile Funding ensures that the work is brought to the people, as opposed to people being handpicked and pulled away from settled teams to form special project teams on demand. Bringing the work to the people means that teams within value streams can settle, become consistent and predictable and move towards becoming high-performing.

This approach can still have a solid governance wrapper; with visibility on progress, transparency on spend and ultimately, clarity in value for money; control is given to the Value Stream and decision-making can be made as close to the customer as possible, and in real-time.

Regular and continuous planning cycles within the value stream, (where budgeting is aligned to its objectives,) reduce the effort and waste involved in continuously requesting and reviewing budgets, freeing up the finance office to focus instead on value outcomes across value streams and long-term financial strategy.

The Five Steps for Value Stream-Based Lean Agile Funding

1. **Objectives and Key Results (OKRs):** Establish OKRs for the Value Stream, aligning strategic goals of the organisation with customer and market needs. Each OKR should include a series of initiatives – where ideas can come from insight, team collaboration and customer feedback

2. **Lean Guardrails for Spend:** Construct a consistent process and policy for spending needs, where short and long-term initiatives can be explored, designed, approved, and managed without friction. Guardrails are essential to ensure that spending decisions are protected and therefore kept frictionless.

3. **Quarterly Value Stream Planning**: Join up and prioritise initiatives across the Value Stream, synchronised against a sprint cycle, ensuring alignment, and gaining regular feedback from the customer.

4. **Build, Measure, Learn:** Get into a cycle of experimentation, measuring and learning what is working.
5. **Visible Success Metrics:** Gain a real-time view of each initiative and its impact on value and spend to enable real-time decision-making.

CHAPTER SEVEN

Building an Agile Organisation

"Speed, agility and responsiveness are the keys to future success."

Anita Roddick

Founder, The Body Shop

I've talked a lot in this book about the culture and mindset change required being the most complex to change. This next section will focus on the practical side, with considerations to be made on the best approach that works for your organisation and needs. Each of these techniques is an introduction and overview only. However, there are plenty of training and coaching materials available through various means to help provide the best support you will need for more in-depth learning and application.

Creating an Agile Culture in Your Organisation

Transforming operations and processes is the easy bit. Transforming the ethos, behaviours and culture of the organisation, as I've mentioned, is really not that easy. But the first step is an acceptance that it needs to change, and that the change is made right at the front door of the Head of the company.

Going back to my survey on trust in Chapter 4. What would you state out of 5 is the level of trust in your organisation, with 5 being Trust and 1 being Fear? As I mentioned, most organisations will believe there is a culture of trust, but when digging a little deeper, the reality is that it is more of a will than a reality. With this in mind, can you honestly say that you have a culture of trust in your organisation?

Have a look at the way teams are given freedom to experiment and innovate. Look at how ideas are generated and followed through. Look at how approvals are made between teams and Management. What autonomy do teams have to make decisions and to take risks? How risk-averse is the organisation? What arrangements are put in place so that employees can learn from mistakes? By having a process, you are making a greater allowance for mistakes to be made and for the growth of the company.

How can you instil a behavioural pattern of trust in your Leadership Team that can be spread across the organisation, where everyone is respectful and fearless for change to happen?

You each have a responsibility to build trust through solidarity, collaboration, empathy and understanding. Spend time together outside the workplace, away from the pressures of the office – it helps, of course, to be co-located, but if not, how can you get together occasionally to build relationships? Think of a newborn baby coming home from the hospital. During a child's life, it will never be seen as so dependent on its parents as it is in those first few days. You will nurture it and be there to support and ensure it has everything it needs. That kind of trust never changes even whilst they are growing up. As a Leadership Team, think about what you would need if you were newborn. Having each other around you to work together is vital inbuilding these foundations and establishing your working relationships and even friendships.

In the book 'Five Dysfunctions of a Team', Lencioni talks about leaders showing their vulnerability in order to build the foundations for trust; a great leap of faith for some, and possibly too big a leap for others. However, it is vital for the good of the company. Think back to the politician taking accountability and saying sorry, and the reaction it got.

It is really important to put together a policy for the organisation of how you would like to operate so that all teams can follow; never set in stone but which helps build accountability in the Leadership Team. For example, innovation. As a Leadership Team, you will have a policy for innovation, and everyone in the organisation would be able to innovate or experiment without fear. Something like that will give a really strong message to the rest of the organisation that it is okay to try, and fail, as long as you learn.

You don't want something like organisational policy to be Draconian or strict, but you do want to encourage a good, respectful and trusting Leadership Team that is accountable, rather than something so relaxed that it is not respected and therefore ignored. A healthy balance is advised, but accountability is key.

You will also want your teams to have their own inter-team charter to protect themselves and also hold each other to account.

In my early days as a Scrum Master at a software company, I used to have a Technical Director who liked to use what we would call "a long-handled screwdriver" to micro-manage teams on the ground, despite the company claiming proudly that they followed Agile practices and allowed for full autonomy amongst its employees.

Most organisations I have worked with in supporting their transformation tend to have a long-handled screwdriver at the Senior Management level in some guise or other. Giving full autonomy to Agile teams is much harder than it sounds, and most Seniors that I work with always believe they give autonomy (no-one ever really admits to micromanaging).

Being autonomous does not only mean defining your own work, but it also includes the creativity involved in solving problems. We are not robots, and complex tasks will involve a level of deliberation, collaboration, and planning in order to execute with quality outcomes. If such complex problems are left to Senior Managers to deal with, all you are creating are human robots who are being programmed according to the organisation's high-level authority.

But what impact can this have on a team where they cannot be fully autonomous? In his book, 'Drive', Daniel Pink states that in order to build motivation in your people, they must have three things (none of which includes money);

Mastery – as in, the right level of knowledge and skill to master their craft.

Autonomy – the freedom to make decisions and create value in their work.

Purpose – a clear and inspiring vision that they can follow; the "why?".

Great leaders will consider all three in equal measure with high value attributed to each one. And motivation is absolutely vital in building high-performing teams. Without it, your teams will tend to have a high turnover of staff, low output, and low value and will be struggling to get out of first gear to build momentum.

Picture an organisation that has motivated people who are fully autonomous, working without fear, free to experiment, continuously evolving, continuously improving, collaborating with each other, working closely with your customers to deliver continuous value, with leaders that support and give freedom and are providing everything that is necessary to make a success for their workforce.

There you have an Agile Organisation.

Mapping Modern Agile Values to Your Company Culture

The original Agile Manifesto was created over 20 years ago with four values that underpinned everything about it, which, at the time and for the best part of those 20 years, were centred around Software Engineering:

- Responding to change over following a plan.
- Individuals and interactions over processes and tools.
- Working software over comprehensive document-ation.
- Customer collaboration over contract negotiation.

Each of these values has helped to change the world of software development, and, to some degree, working practices across an organisation, meaning that they hone right in on being adaptable to change, orientated around people, conversations and cooperation, and most importantly, enable an acute focus on getting software out into the "field" at the earliest opportunity in order to gain fast feedback and enhancement of quality.

For twenty years, the world of IT has benefited from Agile practices in building software in a much smarter way, and these values have driven such revolutionary change. But...

And it's a big BUT...

The values that got us this far in changing the mindset and ways of working in software development limit the potential to establish Agile transformations across the entire organisation.

For a start, it is mostly centred around project delivery, specifically in software, which has created a complex mindset shift where a pre-conceived misconception Agile Coaches hear a lot is, "Agile doesn't apply to us because we are not in IT".

And therefore, the departments outside IT in more traditional companies, perhaps unconsciously, have continued in the same way they have always done, which doesn't entirely support the full tilt needed for transformational change across the organisation.

So, perhaps this is the problem. Because people don't believe it applies to them, transformation is simply something that is required elsewhere, in other parts of the organisation. It doesn't apply to "them".

In her book centred on HR practice, 'Agile People', Pia-Maria Thorén highlights that in order for true Agile transformation to happen right across the company, it isn't simply the way that people work together that solely needs to change, but it is in fact the mindset and therefore a real and proper cultural shift. And because we are talking about mindset, it is essential that HR leaders are the ones involved in driving such change.

But what we need are Agile values that better represent and support transformational change in terms of culture, ways of working and also customer value. In my time as an Agile Coach, I always encouraged leaders to be ambitious; to sever the shackles of risk-averseness and control, and to strive for greatness.

I would challenge them with questions like; "What shape do you want this organisation to take? How far do you want to go? What desire do you have to make real success? Why not be bold?"

The values that got us this far in Agile practice have served their purpose. They got us to change the way that we build and deliver software, and, to some degree, to also change the mindset within the boundaries of IT. However, we need to be bold and ambitious ourselves and really take it to the next level. We need to develop more modern Agile values that are applicable right across the organisation so that everyone can see that transformation really does apply to them and that they can also enable brilliance to achieve real success.

Joshua Kerievsky, CEO of Industrial Logic and the brainchild behind Modern Agile, has created four values to completely remodel Agile practices as a way to focus transformation into being an organisation-wide strategy:

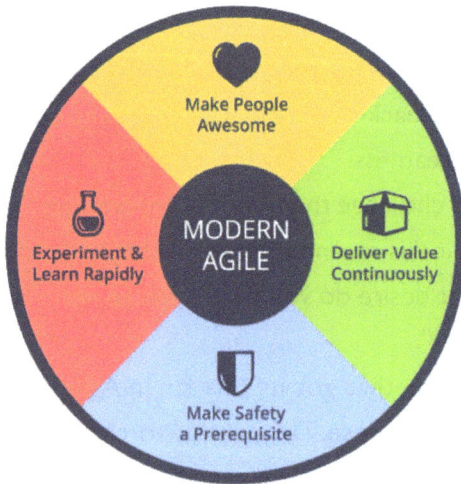

Fig 7.1: Modern Agile: Bringing Agile values up to date

1. **Make people awesome**

Your products and services are reflective of the people you have in the organisation. Therefore, they should be considered your most important commodity, and not profits. This includes everyone from Management, Stakeholders, Teams, and everyone involved. Just as Daniel Pink suggests, motivate people by giving them the autonomy, mastery and purpose that such brilliance can be achieved.

2. **Experiment and learn rapidly**

Innovation should be available at every corner of the organisation, and throughout. Each and every leader and team member should be given the freedom to experiment with ways of working together, the products and services you provide and also its uses internally, thereby creating an environment in which to learn and adapt at pace.

3. **Make safety a pre-requisite**

Safety is born out of the ability to trust with a clear message that it's okay to fail, as long as you learn and adapt. As humans, we need to feel safe in order to thrive in everything that we do. Safety should not be confused with feeling comfortable; this is where complacency can set in and energy and focus can drop. Teams that have psychological safety are able to grow into becoming high-performing as they will be able to trust, create healthy conflict and debate, build commitment, hold each other to account, and become fully outcome-focused, just as Patrick Lencioni describes in his 'Five Dysfunctions' book.

4. **Deliver value continuously**

As has been explained throughout this book, value is the very heart of the organisation and is delivered continuously and includes having a clear purpose in everything that you do and understanding the why. This includes removing all that gets in the way of your teams to establish a tight feedback loop aiming to design, create, deliver and maintain a continuous flow of value.

These four modern Agile values should underpin and drive transformational change, and it starts at the very top. Put together the people you need who can help to steer the transformation in its strategy, and these four values will help to get you started.

There are 12 working principles that are still relevant today and I always encourage teams and leadership to use these to help guide and navigate through transformational change.

Building an Agile culture takes time so start small and don't be afraid to create an environment of openness where you can be honest with each other. This will help you all grow.

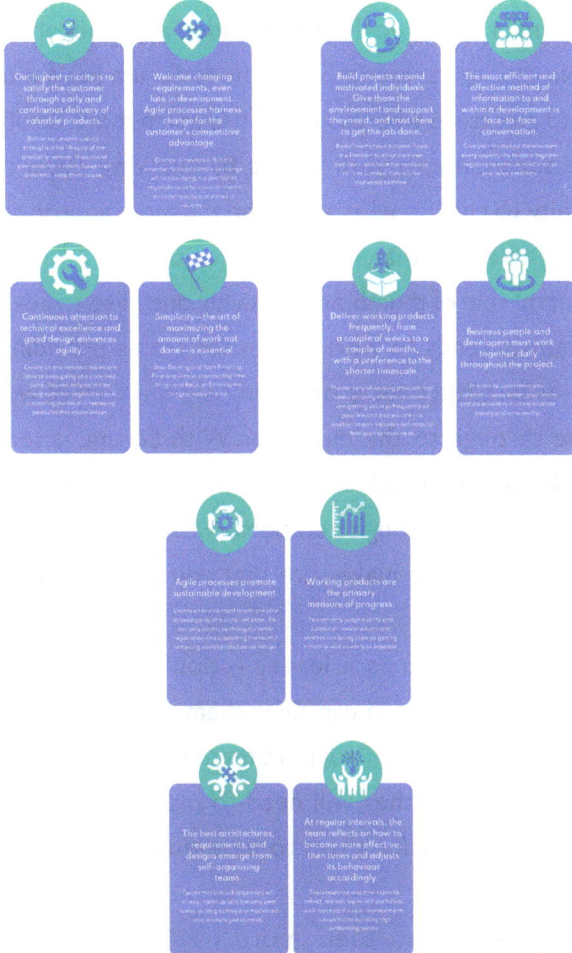

Fig 7.2: Agile Working Principles

Agile Frameworks: Kanban or Scrum

The two main frameworks to consider are Kanban and Scrum. Neither are prescriptive methods: Scrum has a more disciplined structure whereas Kanban is much more flexible.

Give autonomy to your teams by allowing them the opportunity to choose what would be the most appropriate framework to adopt that works best for them.

A general rule of thumb, and certainly one I like to advise, is that Kanban tends to work better for teams providing a service – where the onus is on optimising the flow of work and value through to the customer. With Scrum, it tends to work better for product development teams, where a solution can evolve through iterations, with regular feedback from the customer to make sure that you are building the right product.

A note of caution as a leader – don't dictate which framework a team should use. Give them the autonomy to decide for themselves, but support them by providing them with the information they will need to make that decision and make allowances for them to have time to settle into the practice.

Moving away from their more traditional ways of working as a team towards an Agile framework will require training and some level of coaching, and above all, time. Each member of a team will need to understand the nuances of the chosen framework; its operation, its purpose, and most of all, the terminology involved so that everyone speaks the same language, appreciates the value of the practice that they are taking on, and can also begin the journey fully prepared to make change a success.

Cross-Functional Teams

The simplest definition of a Cross-Functional Team is one in which each of the skills and disciplines that are needed to deliver value is in one group; collaborating, solving problems and most of all, delivering – end to end, with no handoffs to other teams.

More traditional teams will be structured in silos-based skill sets; these include the Design Team, Development Team, Testing Team, and Integration Team. This results in multiple handoffs, approval steps and, ultimately, delays. Project workflows will manoeuvre between each discipline, spending many months in each area. To maintain communication lines, each member of the project team would usually have to attend update meetings, requirement meetings, discovery, etc, even if they haven't been passed the baton. The impact that this level of disruption and context-switching can cause should not be underestimated.

Agile teams cannot really work like this. We have to break down the silos and bring skills together to reduce the level of risk associated with this amount of baton-passing, and also with the lengthy delays in getting value out to the customer.

Cross-functionality ensures that you bring end-to-end skills together, working in close proximity, understanding each other's needs and focusing on quality. If you have a spike in demand, or you lose members of the team unexpectedly, the rest of the team can form a tighter unit to ensure that quality and capability do not drop, and the team doesn't suffer burnout.

There is also a need for expertise in the team – to share knowledge and upskill so that you have a balance of breadth and depth which we call T-Shaped. In software development, a UX Designer does not need to know how to develop code, but has an understanding of the basics. Likewise, an Integration Engineer doesn't need to know how to write automated tests but understands the basic concepts.

Organisations today simply cannot afford to have single points of failure in their teams, where all the knowledge and expertise lies with one person – should anything happen when that person is away, then chaos ensues. People need to feel as though they can take a holiday and truly break away from the demands of their work, safe in the knowledge that the rest of the team are sharing the load. They will come back refreshed, re-energised and ready to go.

When I used to be a Scrum Master, I would always say to any of my team when going on leave. "I don't want to hear from you; go and rest up, leave an 'out of office' on, and we'll see you back in a couple of weeks".

We had to cope, and we usually did. Anyone trying to leave a number to be reached on – "if you need anything, just call me", would usually have to face a forfeit. I'd even have some people offering to be reached when off sick. Go and rest up; we need you back fighting fit.

As business leaders, you have a duty of care to your people. Be aware of their dedication and commitment to their work, but be mindful of what impact that is having on their personal lives and general mental health. This goes back once again to having sustainable teams. Cross-functionality means that whilst there is a breadth of knowledge across the teams, there is also a depth of experience.

There is a myriad of ways in which a team can become T-Shaped; from peer collaboration, to knowledge-sharing sessions, to active learning and so on. But the best thing you can do as a leader is to give them the capacity and time to develop their skills and expertise, just like having the time to settle into Agile practices. This investment and allowance will pay off eventually.

Value Stream Mapping

Value Stream Mapping is designed as a workshop that maps out the full end-to-end process of your product/ service delivery.

As long as you have key leaders in the room who can influence major change, there is a really strong chance you could be able to increase the speed of your end-to-end process by anything from 25 to 75% in just one day. Now, if something takes 2 hours, this isn't going to make huge inroads in and of itself. But if you have an end-to-end process of weeks, even months, then this could be truly transformational for the organisation.

First of all, we need to map out all the steps of the process, i.e., what is involved, who is involved and how long each step takes.

We focus on each step, taking different examples and walking through them.

The second part is then all about stripping out all the unnecessary elements. This is why it is vital for high-level decision-makers to be in the room because, if they have a "chicken in the fight" but are not present, they simply won't buy into the change, and they are the ones who are going to need to make it happen. This cannot be done by proxy.

You would not believe how shocked everyone becomes at the sheer level of waste there is in their processes, how much duplication there is, and how many approvals there are that simply aren't required. It's highly likely the team may never have mapped out their full end-to-end like this before.

Consequently, everyone in the room is then challenged to make it happen, with the highest priority items actioned first.

I have always seen vast transformation come out of these sessions. The best example by far was how I helped the marketing sector of a major communications company improve their campaign delivery timing from 18 months down to just one month by helping them identify areas for automation, and also by reducing duplication and approvals.

The process is by no means easy. It takes great spirit, resolve, courage and an enormous amount of effort in restructuring the organisation toward becoming value-centric.

You will find resistance, but the benefits of building a structure that puts your Product Development Teams and Service Delivery Teams as close to your customers as possible will far outweigh the pain and struggle to get there. Not to mention the great reduction in hidden costs amassed from excessive waste and delays.

Value Stream Management

But it doesn't just stop there. Once you have mapped out and streamlined the pathways of value for your customers, you will then need to implement and manage them going forwards. You will need high-level system thinkers involved in the management of your value streams; those tasked with maintaining and continuously improving the flow of value.

This will include an ongoing task of identifying waste areas, reducing responsibility transference, and monitoring value flow data so as to ensure the organisation is always operating as optimally as possible.

Even if you do nothing else and decide on a different strategy for transforming the company, the concept of Value Streams can be adopted anywhere with great gains for the organisation and is most highly recommended as an essential strategic priority.

Why Transformation Fails

Failure is an unfortunate yet common outcome of transformation. I would love to tell you that simply following this book will give you all you need to know about Agile adoption. However, there are some common pitfalls, and if you are not careful, you could very easily fall into its traps. I have seen transformations fail in a number of organisations I have worked with, and I can guarantee you that you are most certainly at risk of failure due to at least one of the following five common reasons, all of which are avoidable:

1. **Lack of management commitment:** I am always intrigued when I see a lack of commitment in transformation. Why invest in major business change and then turn your focus and dedication to other priorities? Maybe the reason is due to the lack of

belief that there is a problem in the first place, and if there is, that it is not big enough to justify the level of investment required. Or it could be the misconception that Management are not required to change, and therefore, (without realising) they actually end up hindering progress. Or it could be that some levels of Management are not convinced that this is the right solution and simply go through the motions to show minimal commitment to avoid losing face. Or it could be a combination of all three. But more often than not, it is the principal killer of a successful adoption of Agile practice. A telling sign for me of lack of commitment is when Management are unable to find the time, or book time in and then cancel late or at the last minute. There are always greater priorities at play, and in the end, the entire transformational process is at risk.

2. **Lack of trust:** As mentioned many times in the book already, trust is the foundation on which your transformation must be built. Typical reasons could include:

   i) lack of trust in Agile as a practice: the disbelief that it is the right direction for the organisation and that the level of the problem may not warrant the level of investment in time and resources needed.

ii) lack of trust in the people to help make the change, perhaps stemming from a similar mindset that prevents them from taking risks in the company.

iii) a lack of innovation and delegation of responsibility.

iv) where command and control leadership behaviour is rife.

3. **Unrealistic expectations:** Transformation takes time, and it doesn't follow a smooth or straight path. Sending your people on a training course and expecting them to become an Agile force straight off the bat is not realistic. Settled, high-performing teams need several months working consistently together, with sufficient space and time, plenty of support, little disruption, and few high demands to become a success. An investment made now should be made with an acceptance that teams need time and a reduction in the level of demands made, with an understanding that the fruits of this investment will be realised in time when demands can increase.

The Virginia Satir's Change Model shown in Fig (7.3) below shows the typical journey that organisations take in any change process.

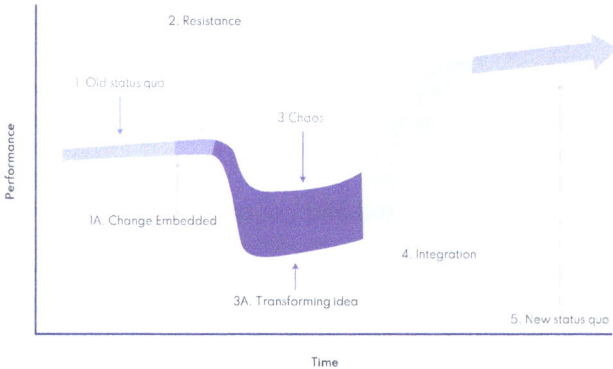

Fig 7.3: Virginia Satir's Change Model

Chaos and integration are the most complex and challenging of phases, and the areas in which transformation is more than likely to fail. It is the area where expectations can completely misalign with the reality of change, and therefore, patience could run out and added pressures could cause old ways and behaviours to return.

What the model doesn't represent is time, as it will be different for each organisation and for each change requirement. Therefore, it is essential that you don't compare the length of time it takes with anyone else but be safe in the knowledge that it will take a considerable amount of time.

4. **Insufficient Agile experience and skills:** Senior leaders who try to go it alone and change the culture and ways of working of the company without Agile and Transformation coaches and consultants working with teams and leadership tend to struggle – existing, hidden problems will continue to fester and teams and management will become frustrated and disillusioned, and sadly, will revert to what they are most familiar in doing, where they feel safe. Experienced Agile expertise at each level of the organisation needs to be in place to drive the change on the ground. Without this, the process simply leads to inconsistent practice, misunderstandings, and misinterpretations of how it is all supposed to work.

    What tends to happen is the realisation that support is required, and so Coaches and Consultants are brought in halfway through. They then have a real challenge to reverse the damage caused by not having the right expertise in place at the outset, and usually have to start by unpicking some of the bad habits that have sneaked in. Either that or Agile is blamed outright for the problems at play; the initial problems that required change in the first place have not been fixed, and so old ways and behaviours return and Management simply throw in the towel.

You would never completely renovate a house without having the right expertise in place to ensure its success. You wouldn't try going it alone with a couple of mates and a few trips down to the DIY store. In an extremely short time, you would realise that you most certainly need to bring in an architect to help design it, a building contractor firm to carry out the major building works, and perhaps an interior designer to help you furnish your property to your liking.

Because you are dealing with many people, having a community of Agile expertise, through Coaches and players, will give you a much stronger foundation for success.

5. **Resistance to change:** Some people may simply be resistant, unwilling and just don't share the same vision and desire to transform. Instead, and perhaps

unconsciously, they become a disruption and therefore prevent progress – possibly out of fear of their own position, or maybe from lack of faith in the realistic chances of success, or perhaps from a lack of patience in the process. This could happen at any level within the company, and your responsibility as a leader is to identify those that are resistant and possibly disruptive and find a way in which you can find a suitable outcome for both parties. Some may eventually get on board; they simply prefer to take their time and need to build confidence in taking the step. However, some may never get there, and honest and frank conversations may therefore be required.

Fundamentally, how a transformation could fail all comes down to a lack of real leadership, that is all.

What it really takes is:

- strong, committed leaders, with a real willingness to show vulnerability to help build trust.
- leaders who make allowances for teams to adapt their working practice with sufficient time by setting out clear expectations.
- investment into getting the right Agile training and coaching support to work with teams.

- the leadership to help transform, ensuring consistency across the company.
- the commitment to identify those who may not share the same vision, direction, and desire with a view to finding a suitable resolution.
- the real willingness to change across the organisation, not just in the way that people work, but also the whole ethos and culture of the organisation.

Once again, I stress, you must put some time aside to look inward and ask the questions about your commitment, willingness, and your own desire to not just make the change for the good of the organisation, but to be a true leader and strong champion for the change.

CHAPTER EIGHT

Getting Started on the Road to Optimum Business Agility

*"As a leader the first person I need to lead is me. The
first person that I should try to change is me."*
John C Maxwell
Author

The Agilistic Business Agility Transformation Framework™

No large-scale transformation can ever be successful without following some sort of framework. And just like in Agile practice, we say framework as opposed to method, as we cannot prescribe specifically what you need to do as a step-by-step process. Instead, we suggest a framework to work within to adapt to the needs and make-up of the organisation.

There are four key stages in the Agilistic transformation framework. Each is vital to ensure success, and it is advised not to cut corners. Yes, you could try going it alone, without support – but eventually, you will reach a stage where, without the right skills and expertise in place, you will struggle to embed the very principles and values that Agile promotes, and your teams will end up reverting back to what they know best.

The techniques within this framework have been tried and tested across many organisations and transformations:

- **The Agile Launch Pad –** Senior Leadership Transformation Foundations
- **Phase One –** Testing Through a Pilot
- **Phase Two –** Scaling Agile across the Organisation
- **Phase Three –** Tipping Point to Transform the Organisation

Fig 8.1: Agilistic Business Agility Transformation Framework™

The Agile Launch Pad

Changing the way an organisation is structured, its culture, its way of working, and, at the same time, delivering value to its customers takes time and a high degree of commitment, especially from Senior Management (as mentioned earlier – this is the main crux of this book!).

This level of commitment is no more vital than in the pre-phase of the framework. What we ask of you, as a leader, is that you clear your diary for four days and get away from the office. Together with the rest of your team, you will need time, headspace, and deep focus to create the foundations for change. It should not be underestimated and should certainly not be delegated. Therefore, it needs to be given top priority ahead of everything else. You need to consider it as the best time investment you could give to the organisation this year, or possibly ever.

Over the four days, you will not only set out a plan and strategy for the transformation; you will embark on a journey of discovery for the art of the possible. You will be challenged in many areas; from the value you give to your customers, to thinking differently about how you operate as an organisation, to the very culture of the company and what steps you are going to need to take to change.

Day One – Assess:

Business Agility Baseline Assessment

Before you start on the journey, you need to assess your current agility levels to set a baseline.

This might sound a little crazy; to assess your own business agility before you've started becoming an Agile Organisation. But in actual fact, it will give you key areas to focus on for improvement in the initial stages.

The assessment will focus on all four pillars of the organisation:

- People and Culture (including Leadership)
- Technology and Tools
- Process and Governance
- Structure and Environment

Each member of your Senior Leadership Team (SLT) should take the assessment in unison, answering a series of questions related to each pillar, where they themselves can provide their own view on the organisation's current agility status.

An average rating score will be given to each pillar along with areas to develop.

It is imperative that everyone taking the assessment is given a chance to provide openness and honesty. This is the starting point for change. Accepting that there is a problem in some areas will help you all to clear the path for transformation. There may be some that become quite defensive, especially if it is focused on their own area. Agile is a powerful tool to hold up a mirror to the organisation, and occasionally, people are not too comfortable with the reflection of what they see. You will need to be mindful that this is a natural response to change and that only from acceptance will there be an opportunity for positive change.

Day Two – Value Focus:

Day two is all about focusing on value; reviewing the main purpose of the organisation, and identifying clear measures of success against the value that you deliver to your customers.

Creating Objectives and Key Results (OKRs) – Measurable Outcomes Workshop

How will you determine success? How will you measure it?

It is vitally important to stress that the measure of your success should not be based on any corporate number that has been set as a sales target for the year. Rather, it should be against the level of value delivered to your customers. That is the rich data that will help you as an organisation transform towards becoming Value-Centric.

Arrange a workshop to bring together senior leaders, stakeholders and product owners to determine the measure of success.

The workshop should be conducted with a blank canvas and facilitated in a way that enables clear, open discussion on what it is that will establish clear success criteria.

When I've run this workshop in the past, I have taken the following steps to get the group to a position of clarity:

- **Why:** Everyone in the room considers the purpose of the organisation, product, service and what value it brings to its customers. What are the problems that are solved?
- **Who:** Who is impacted by the products and services that the organisation provides and what are the typical personas?
- **Identify Clear Objectives:** What is it that the organisation would like to achieve?

- **Identify Measurable Outcomes – Key Results:** What are the key measures that will determine success, with the following criteria;
  - ¤ Name – *for reference*
  - ¤ Value – *what value will the outcome bring to the organisation?*
  - ¤ Scale – *typically % or #*
  - ¤ Method – *how will the measure be captured, and can it be automated?*
  - ¤ Baseline – *what is the current measure (if applicable)?*
  - ¤ Target – *what is a realistic target, set over a 3–6-month period?*
- **Review and Identify Initiatives:** What are the existing initiatives at play or imminent? Do they align with the OKRs? Are they prioritised or de-prioritised accordingly? What ideas do the Product Owners (and their teams) have that could help move the dial of their Measurable Outcomes?

Following on from the workshop, some work will be required. Many organisations I have worked with use it as a tick-box exercise and don't allow sufficient time to really embed the measures into working practice.

Remember the 6 key factors in creating quality OKRs:

1. Measurable
2. Simplicity
3. Team Control
4. Complete Alignment
5. Review Regularly
6. Visibility and Live

How can the data be automated and fed directly into a live, visible system where, at any point, anyone from the business can see the level of value that is being provided to your customers, and of course how successful your initiatives are?

I would recommend running this type of workshop as part of a review every quarter and allowing sufficient time for your teams to link their own OKRs directly up to executive level.

Day Three – Transform:

Day three is where we start to look at the overall structure and operation.

Value Stream Identification Workshop

We start off by helping the SLT to identify key value streams in the organisation (as mentioned in the Creating a Value-Centric Organisation chapter).

NB: This is not to map value streams at this stage. We will need more time and specialist members of your staff for mapping which can take a number of days to complete.

Our focus during the Launch Pad will be to identify how value moves through the organisation and what a future state could look like, and we will take the following steps:

1. Group and categorise your products and services.
2. Outline support networks that exist for your products and service teams, e.g., HR, Finance, Operations, 3rd parties, etc.
3. Identify Value Streams based on horizontal slicing from end to end.
4. Conduct an initial walk-through to make sure which slice would be most appropriate for a test pilot.
5. Plan out the next stage which includes Value Stream Mapping. This will be done back at the office with key specialists and decision-makers.

It is worth mentioning that your existing organisational structure may not fit perfectly with the flow of value to your customers. Therefore, you will need to consider the enthusiasm of the SLT to make wholesale structural changes. This discussion can happen during the workshop, but some pre-thinking/discussion is recommended. You want to avoid arriving at this workshop without having had the discussion as a group. At the same time, it will be beneficial not to arrive with all of the answers as this may cloud your best judgement. There will be plenty of opportunity to reach the best outcomes for the organisation in this space. Therefore, any pre-discussion should be limited to simply aligning on the need to restructure for the benefit of becoming a value-centric organisation.

Leadership Kanban Workshop

We then set up a live Kanban Board to help provide a visual structure, and a task board for the transformation process.

The board will be split into the four categories – People, Process, Technology and Structure – and will follow a workflow of tasks towards completion, encapsulated within a working and dynamic system.

Everything that is going on at leadership level will need to be illustrated on this board. Every escalation that comes into the team will be defined here and will provide clear transparency and focus for progress.

If your teams see what you are doing to do to impact change, they will be more likely to follow suit.

Note: This is not a tick-box exercise! It is imperative that the Kanban system is implemented and kept active; this way, you will be able to have impactful conversations amongst your peers with a dynamic visual aid.

During the workshop, we run through scenarios and identify disparities to fill and problems to solve. We will establish typical items to go on the Leadership Kanban Board *and how it will be managed going forward. The growth plan from day one will go on the board, and we continue to add items to it for the rest of the week (and beyond, of course).

Day Four – Strategy:

The final day of the Agile Launch Pad is to create a plan and strategy for change. This is the most important day; the

---

* *See The Agile Operation chapter for further details on Leadership Kanban* outcomes of this day will set out the path towards optimum Business Agility for the organisation.

We look at the structure of the Senior Leadership Team; how the function of the Chief Executive Office is currently set up for Agility, and what will need to change; i.e., how each C-Suite area can become fully optimised and how each Chief x Officer (CxO) can lead the organisation through the transformation as a fully cross-functional Office. We look at how to ensure effective communication and visibility can exist in the current structure and how – including the assembly of communities and early adopters. We will look at the finance model, i.e., how new initiatives are funded, how we can adopt a leaner, more agile way of funding new initiatives that maintains the necessary levels of governance but removes unnecessary approvals and waste.

We create a strategy for testing out Agile practices with a Pilot Team before the organisation is able to scale these practises across the company. We look at what training and coaching support is required. What will they need to do to set things in motion?

And finally, we look at the next steps – planning out the next 12 weeks and taking the insights from the week and implementing the master plan.

Maintaining Momentum:

After four days of intense, strategic planning and deep focus, the organisation will be ready to take the leap of faith towards transforming the organisation. But be careful; the role of the leader is not done here. You will still need to actively participate and support your people throughout. Be mindful that it could be very easy to revert back to the norm once back in the daily grind. Therefore, you will need to carve out some periods of time to follow up, as well as dedicating time, focus and most of all energy into making sure it happens. You will not be the first to get to three months, not see very much change and look back and regret a missed opportunity. The best time to act is immediately. We always say, make a commitment of the four days, but also make sure to dedicate follow-on time once you are back in the office.

Your workforce will be expecting to hear from you and will be wondering what is going on. Make sure to allow time to communicate the strategy and set expectations. Focus on internal PR and create a safe space for people to come and ask questions. One recommendation would be to create a community of those who may be enthused to help shape the transformation and get involved in the early stages; we call this an early adopter community. This shouldn't just be limited to "early adopters" but a place for discussions and answers for all. Be mindful that rumours spread very quickly. People will be most concerned about what the change is going to mean for them. They would have heard rumours about how Agile doesn't need certain roles. Therefore, some of your employees will quickly become fearful of their own position in the company. You will need to reassure them that they still have a place if they are willing to get on side and that there will be support available. Your HR team will be vital in this regard, as will the vision that you set and the energy and enthusiasm that you bring.

Support Groups

The following are levels of support to help move you towards becoming a Value-Centric company:

- **Role-Based Communities** – *Agile-specific roles within the Value Stream; Scrum Masters / Kanban Leads, Product Owners, Agile Leadership. An opportunity to focus on best practice, highlight and solve common issues and generally ensure consistency across the organisation for each role.*

- **Agile Communities** – *A viewpoint from different angles in the business of Agile practice in general and how it is and isn't working in certain areas. Highlighting and solving problems and generally ensuring consistency across the organisation for Agile practice.*
- **Team of Teams Escalation and Support** – *These groups will be set up according to the Product or Service area (value stream) as a means to support each team, with a clear escalation route and clear visibility of everything that is going on in that area.*
- **Functional Area Chapters** –*These groups are set up to share best practice and raise any common issues of specific functional lines across multiple teams; for example, designers, data analysts, and creative marketing. Not to be confused with reporting lines.*

For each of these groups, it is imperative to have a working agreement across the membership that includes how often each group should get together, and that there are clear outcomes and ownership. Each group should also have visibility of their work for clarity and transparency as well.

To guarantee success, each Value Stream and Product Development/Service Delivery Team should be well supported with sufficient Agile knowledge and experience within each.

Phase One: The Pilot Phase

The first phase we enter will be to run a test pilot for three months. Ideally, you can bring together a dedicated team of cross-functional skills and be given a problem to solve. The team will need to be low-key and low-risk – meaning they will need to be isolated from business as usual and the pressures of delivery and corporate demands. The reason for this is that if they are under any sort of pressure to deliver, or if they are exposed to general, daily demands from Management outside the training environment, they will become distracted, and you will risk losing the quality of benefits that an Agile Pilot Team can give you.

How you form the team will determine the level of rich data you will be able to collate that will be used to scale across the organisation. The prime objective for the Pilot Team will be to learn how Agile can be implemented into the organisation. Any value outcomes delivered to your customers should be considered a bonus.

So, keep the problem to solve simple, realistic, and most of all, independent of external teams or even 3rd parties, enabling the team to deliver value end-to-end without disruption or delay.

You should expect there to be some honest and candid conversations. Therefore, encouragement of your "pilot players" to provide a picture of reality is paramount. Whilst the Pilot Team will be testing out Agile practices, a steer should be given to look at the four areas of escalation and ensure there is available leadership to support; People, Process, Technology and Structure.

Any new team that is formed in the organisation should follow a consistent process of onboarding and it is no different for your Pilot Team.

Agile Training: It is imperative that every member of the Pilot Team is given training to understand the practice and principles, but also to make sure that everyone is on the same page and speaking the same language. Even if you have some members with experience, it's always useful to align with those that do not. Also, it always helps to have people on the team with experience.

Measurable Outcomes Workshop: What is the problem that the team will solve? Who will benefit? And what is the measure of success?

Ideation Workshop: What initiatives will help the team achieve success?

Ways of Working Workshop: How will the team work together? What will their general policies be? This session will be to help formulate a working agreement that will help to hold each other to account.

Planning and Kick-Off: And finally, planning for the next couple of weeks, and a formal launch to help build momentum and energy. Stakeholders should be encouraged to attend the launch ceremony so that they can feel part of the team, if not full-time and dedicated.

As with all Agile teams, your Pilot Team should include a **Scrum Master (SM)** with the main objectives to be supporting the team from within, identifying/ helping to remove impediments, and ensuring they have everything they need to manage their day-to-day operation. This includes facilitating key Agile events as well as the tools and processes that they will be working with. Ideally, your SM will be experienced in the role so is able to hit the ground running. Your SM will be the most valuable member of the Pilot Team for it is they who will help you identify what problems will need solving prior to scaling.

Your Pilot Team should also include a **Product Owner (PO)**. This person will be focused on value outcomes and can help communicate the work to the team. The PO will help bring an understanding of the process of User Stories, iterative development and bringing regular feedback to the team. Again, ideally, the PO will be experienced in the role and can therefore leave the focus on Agile learning for the rest of the team. In the instance of the pilot, the onus will be less on value delivery, but more on Agile practices – therefore, the PO should be less focused on delivery and more on embedding good principles and practice in the early stages.

Over the period of the pilot, the team should follow good Agile Scrum principles of working within a two-week iterative sprint, gathering regularly for a **daily stand-up** to align on the work and raise any impediments. Invite Stakeholders in for a regular **sprint review** and feedback, *circa* every two weeks, and most importantly, focus on continuously improving with a **team retrospective**, before **sprint planning** for the next 2 weeks.

You may wish to put together a forum group and/or an "early adopter" community of practice as an opportunity for representatives from the pilot (as well as others in the business) to help shape the scaling of Agile practice, in addition to solving organisation-wide problems identified in the pilot.

Three months should be sufficient time to learn where the most challenging blockers are and to give you an opportunity to solve some problems prior to being ready to scale. You may be tempted to roll out sooner than three months, and if you are ready, then that is fine. However, my recommendation is to identify what readiness looks like prior to starting. Be warned – scaling too soon will result in you carrying the same problems across the organisation, but with the added challenge then of having to solve them on a grander scale; like trying to change a tyre on a moving vehicle.

Phase Two: Scaling Agile Across the Organisation

Scaling is going to be your greatest challenge in the transformation. This is the point at which your role as a leader is going to be really tested. The simple option would be to go back to your old ways because the wolf is too close to the door as you try to navigate a full-scale transformation whilst also trying to keep the business running.

I have been involved in numerous transformations, and I have to say, scaling has been the one area where organisations tend to struggle the most – most notably because either not enough support and experience is brought in, and the "business as usual" work tends to trump any activity that will help the organisation to scale.

Both aspects can of course be mitigated, but it takes great will and a degree of acceptance that the road will be rocky for a while, and as long as you can take the hit, the gold at the end of the rainbow will be greatly stocked.

So how do you scale effectively? First of all, you need to be careful not to simply take an off-the-shelf scaling model like Scaled Agile Framework (SAFe), The Spotify engineering framework, or Large-Scale Scrum (LeSS) that you feel would fit perfectly into the organisation. Each has its merits and can work, but I would be very cautious about bringing in something like this and making it fit. Tempting as it may be, with all the answers readily available, it can so easily be over-engineered, and it subsequently may not be quite what you need.

My recommendation is to consider the following four areas against the diagram below, and adapt into an operational model that could work for you:

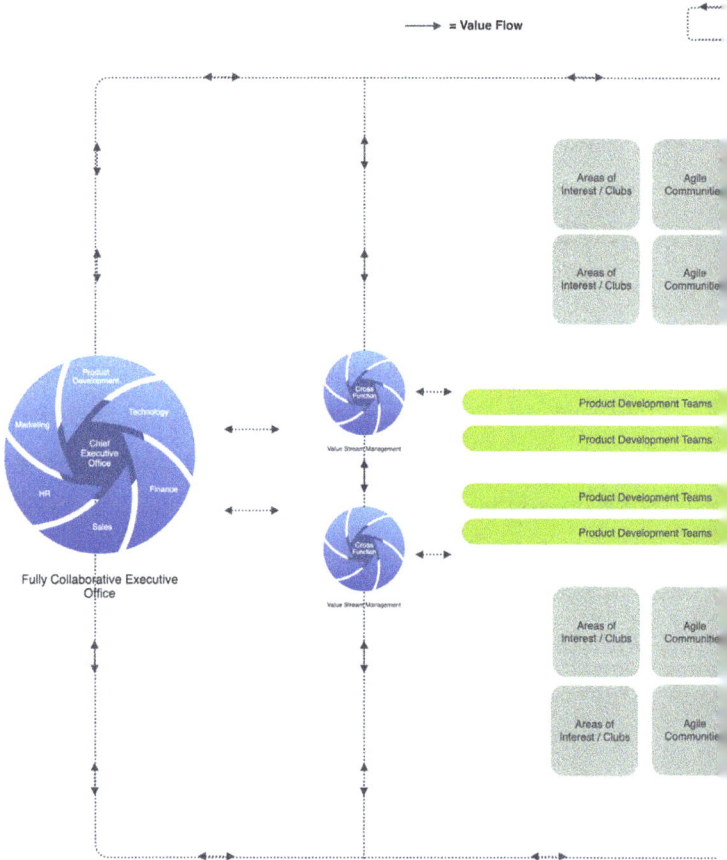

⟶ = Value Flow

Areas of Interest / Clubs

Agile Communities

Areas of Interest / Clubs

Agile Communities

Cross Function

Value Stream Management

Product Development Teams

Product Development Teams

Product Development Teams

Product Development Teams

Product Development

Technology

Marketing

Chief Executive Office

Finance

HR

Sales

Fully Collaborative Executive Office

Cross Function

Value Stream Management

Areas of Interest / Clubs

Agile Communities

Areas of Interest / Clubs

Agile Communities

eedback Loops   ◄····► = Communication Flow

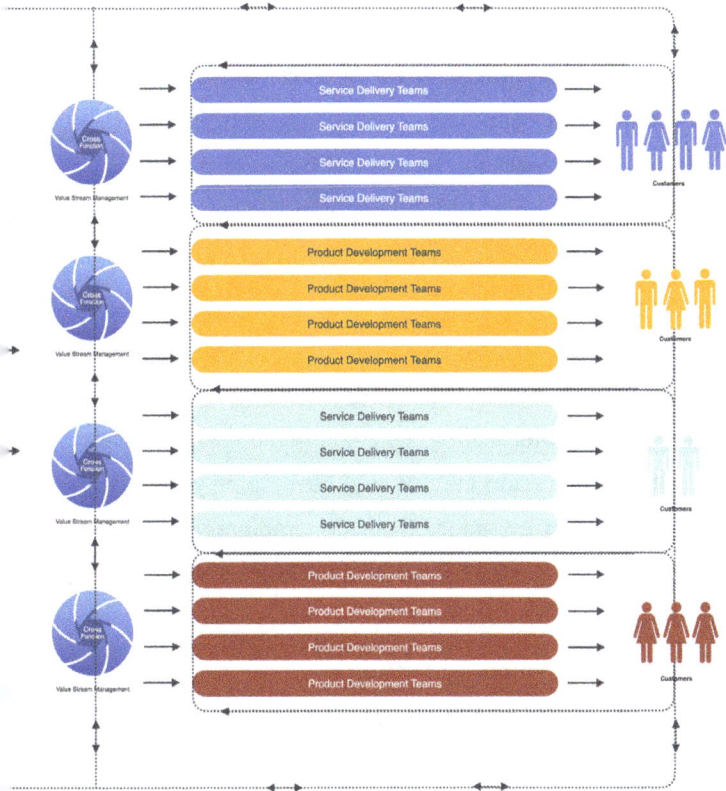

Cross Function

Value Stream Management

Service Delivery Teams
Service Delivery Teams
Service Delivery Teams
Service Delivery Teams

Customers

Product Development Teams
Product Development Teams
Product Development Teams
Product Development Teams

Customers

Service Delivery Teams
Service Delivery Teams
Service Delivery Teams
Service Delivery Teams

Customers

Product Development Teams
Product Development Teams
Product Development Teams
Product Development Teams

Customers

Value: Throughout this book, I've mentioned: -

i) how you will need to transform the company to become Value-Centric.

ii) how the way you scale will need to have this mindset at the forefront.

iii) how the structure will need to be centred around value and how rapidly you can deliver this value directly to your customers.

This means breaking down the silos and getting your Product Development and Service Delivery Teams as close to the customer as possible. Scaling Agile will mean re-structuring, changing behaviours and culture, and developing your teams to be fully focused on value. Consider implementing Value Streams to bring a clear flow of continuous value from inception of idea through to delivery and response.

Lines of Communication: Traditional companies rely heavily on reporting and regular meetings to ensure lines of communication are clear and understood. This, however, causes great stress and a mismanaged use of time. In the new world of Agile, however, the way we communicate has changed, and most certainly for the better. We use live visibility and transparency to communicate. We have structured proceedings that each team will run which help them to communicate with strength and clarity, whilst implementing a structured and effective escalation path up the chain. All the work taking place in the organisation, across each value stream, escalation and Upper Management, should be visible, transparent and accessible – therefore ensuring the lines of communication remain free-flowing, effective and most of all, efficient.

Structure: The structure here is key. You will see in the diagram that the Value Stream model includes a support arm that manages the flow; making sure that each stream is clear, providing value continuously and making sure the feedback loop is tight. How big you make the management arm will vary greatly. It is advised that you avoid top-loading, rather putting the hands-on resource into the Value Streams and minimising Management to focus on supporting the streams and looking beyond the horizon as mentioned earlier in the book.

Process: The pattern of planning in small increments, designing, development, testing and delivering, getting feedback, and adapting, responding, and repeating the cycle can be easily scaled as long as the communication lines are there. Some Agile organisations like to plan as a collective across multi-teams to ensure consistency, reduce duplicated effort, maintain communication lines, and also remove any dependencies. I would consider this a viable option but try not to overcomplicate it. Make sure you have the people necessary in the room, and sufficient time is dedicated to achieving the best outcomes. It is more appropriate to plan in big chunks across multiple teams every quarter or so and leave small incremental planning to each team on a more regular basis.

Just as in the onboarding of the Pilot Team, the same will apply to each new Agile Product Development or Service Delivery Team:

Agile Training: It is imperative that every member of the team is given training to understand the practice and principles, but also to make sure that everyone is on the same page and speaking the same language. Even if you have some members with experience, it's always useful to align with those that do not. Plus, it always helps to have people on the team with experience.

Measurable Outcomes Workshop: What is the problem that the team will solve? Who benefits? What is the measure of success?

Ideation Workshop: What initiatives will help the team achieve success?

Ways of Working Workshop: How will the team work together? What will their general policies be? This session will be to help formulate a working agreement that will help hold each person accountable.

Planning and Kick-Off: Finally planning for the forthcoming couple of weeks, and a formal kick-off to help build momentum and energy. Stakeholders should be encouraged to attend the launch event so that they can feel part of the team (if not full-time) and dedicated.

Support Groups

The following are levels of support to help move you towards becoming a Value-Centric company:

- **Role-Based Communities** – *Agile-specific roles within the Value Stream; Scrum Masters / Kanban Leads, Product Owners, Agile Leadership. An opportunity to focus on best practice, highlight and solve common issues and generally ensure consistency across the organisation for each role.*

- **Agile Communities** – *A viewpoint from different angles in the business of Agile practice in general and how it is and isn't working in certain areas. Highlighting and solving problems and generally ensuring consistency across the organisation for Agile practice.*

- **Team of Teams Escalation and Support** – *These groups will be set up according to the Product or Service area (value stream) as a means to support each team, with a clear escalation route and clear visibility of everything that is going on in that area.*

- **Functional Area Chapters –***These groups are set up to share best practice and raise any common issues of specific functional lines across multiple teams; for example, UX designers, data analysts, and creative marketing. Not to be confused with reporting lines.*

For each of these groups, it is imperative to have a working agreement across the membership that includes how often each group should get together, and that there are clear outcomes and ownership. Each group should also have visibility of their work for clarity and transparency as well.

To guarantee success, each Value Stream and Product Development/Service Delivery Team should be well supported with sufficient Agile knowledge and experience within each.

Agile Training

It is highly recommended that your Leadership Team go on a specialist Agile Leadership Training course together. You will then be able to take what you've learnt in this book to the next level of understanding and knowledge. Ideally, this should happen prior to the Agile Launch Pad event.

As you scale, each of your teams should get an intro to Agile training and also either Kanban or Scrum training according to what is appropriate. Product Development Teams usually go for Scrum whilst most other teams, like Operations, would benefit from Kanban, based on workflow. However, there is no strict rule, and some teams can even combine the two. My advice is to give teams the option rather than be prescriptive. Good Agile Trainers should be versatile enough to adapt their training accordingly.

Most Agile Foundations Training (both for Leaders and also Teams) are about two days in duration.

There are also specialist types of roles in Agile. The two main ones are Product Owners and Scrum Masters/Kanban Leads. The basics are the Product Owners who will represent the customer, ensuring a direct link with the team, with a tight feedback loop and the management of the backlog of requirements which we call user stories.

The Scrum Master/Kanban Lead is the facilitator of the team and will do all they can to clear the path for success.

Neither of these roles are management roles; each member of the team is on the same level, with varying degrees of experience.

This is essential. In order for a team to thrive, it must have no conflict of management hierarchy. Instead, there should be a clear vision, with each member working together towards fulfilling it.

Who you decide should take on these roles is particularly significant. Some organisations will believe that Project Managers and Product Managers can easily take them on. This isn't always the case, and I would be careful in choosing who would be most suitable.

The main type of people to consider are those who have no ego, who will serve the team, who will work in collaboration and respect their peers as an equal and most of all, can be fully focused on helping the team to become high-performing.

Once you have these roles assigned, you can put them on specialist trainings; i.e., the Certified Scrum Master CSM or Kanban Practitioner course is industry standard, as is the Certified Product Owner CPO. For more details on these roles, consider Geoff Watts' Product Mastery and Scrum Mastery books where he provides a great working guide on the specific roles.

Agile Coaching and Mentoring

The role of the Agile Coach, and generally coaching within an organisation, is very much a recent addition to the landscape of business enterprise, and so some people can still be a little wary of the value and impact that a coach can have.

There are two specific aims for the coach. One is to support each team and help them build the foundations of agility and settle into a sustainable rhythm of predictability. The Coach will also oversee and facilitate the initial

193

onboarding phase. The Coach's other aim is to help the team to think differently about how they deliver value, breaking down the work and closing the feedback loop tight by getting regular feedback as they evolve the product or service.

The Coach will work closely with the Scrum Master/ Kanban Lead and Product Owner to help them to grow into the role, using mentorship and facilitation skills for these key roles to follow. Experienced Agile Coaches will have a wealth of Agile knowledge and a varied range of techniques to help each team to adapt to their own practice.

Most Coaches will also work at Management level to help bridge the gaps between the teams and to support the growth and experience levels of Agile leaders in the organisation.

The role of the Agile Coach should not be underestimated and is certainly one which you really cannot do without during the Pilot and Scaling of Agile into the organisation. You may also consider bringing in an Enterprise Coach who will be positioned at the Senior Leadership level. They will help coach and mentor Senior leaders in the role, supporting the implementation and execution of Agile Transformation across the organisation. Remember, you as a leader will need to be fully immersed in the programme, therefore, having coaching support is vital.

Your strategy for Scaling, coupled with how quickly you want or need to transform the organisation should determine how many Coaches you will need. A good Agile Team Coach should be able to work with 2-3 teams at any one point and should require around 12 weeks to get the team off the ground. If you have experienced Scrum Masters inside the teams, then this should help, but it is not a case of either/or. The Agile Coach will have a focus at a higher level than the Scrum Master, identifying issues beyond the team, though the two should complement each other to build foundations for the team.

The Agile Coach can also help facilitate the communities and support groups in the early stages to get them off the ground.

The third aim of the Agile Team Coach and Enterprise Agile Coach should always be to eventually leave the organisation so there is full independence and sufficient knowledge and experience inside. This should really be the tipping point for the engagement, and one of the measures of success the Coaches will have.

Here are some points to consider carefully. Over recent years, the role has become very popular. There is no real regulation for good, strong Agile Coaching – and so there is always a risk of not getting good value for money. Be mindful of Coaches coming in at cut-price. The best ones I have worked with are the ones who have the experience in multiple different industries over a number of years.

The other thing to consider is that the Coach should not be an employee of the organisation. The author of 'Coaching Agile Teams', Lyssa Adkins says, "you don't want career-threatening conversations".

The Coach will need to stand aside from the company, away from the politics and day-to-day stresses, to clearly see where the main issues are, and be in a strong position to have conversations at multiple levels of Management without repercussions and which will enable greater improvements. If the Coach is an employee, then this comes with extra challenges which you will neither have time for, nor is it something you would want to risk.

Phase Three: Business Agility Transformation

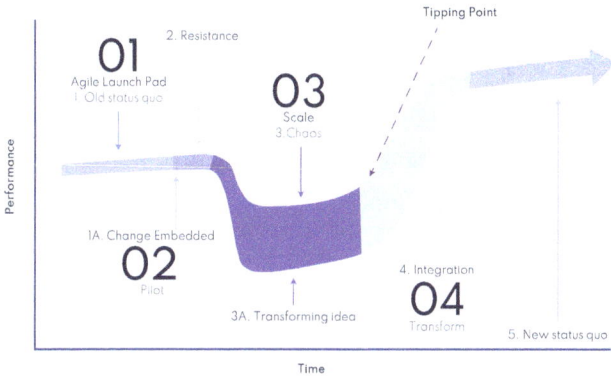

Fig 8.2: Virginia Satir's Change Model combined with the Agilistic Framework

Based on your scaling strategy, the tipping point of transformation should be reached just about the time when the majority of teams and restructuring have been embedded and practising Agile where organisational issues have been ironed out and managed. This is when you will start to see some real momentum and great benefit.

This could take anywhere between 6-24 months and is very much dependent on the size of the organisation, the starting position, and the number of teams to scale.

This isn't to say that you won't already recognise or experience improvements during this time. On the contrary, you should start seeing some real progress even in the Pilot Phase. However, the major change won't happen until you get to a stage where the old status quo is well and truly behind you as an organisation, and the familiarity with Agile practice starts to become second nature across multiple teams and Value Streams.

Each executive office – Finance, HR, Information, Product, Service, Operations, Marketing, Sales and Technology – will begin to be fully collaborative and cross-functional, where silos have completely crashed down and a new circular loop will have formed.

The operation across the organisation will have reached a point of optimisation and each Value Stream and support will be fully focused on continuing to improve even further.

In this way, new initiatives, new products and services, and maintaining and upgrading old ones will have completely changed, whilst maintaining governance, but removing delays and waste.

The culture within the organisation will be one of trust and accountability, focusing on value outcomes. A buzz will have risen, and everyone in the organisation will be looking for new ways to solve problems and experiment. The mindset will have shifted to such a degree that there will be a momentum shift in the way that the organisation and its people think and collaborate, focusing on the continuous delivery of value.

Teams will have started to become high-performing and fully responsive to their customers, ensuring a tightly closed feedback loop.

You may think it sounds like utopia, and possibly consider asking the question "is it all worth it?". You can be forgiven for thinking that way. I have not exactly pulled any punches throughout the book. Yes, it is really hard, complex and thoroughly challenging. It may take longer and cost more than you think. You will lose people along the way; good people, some of whom may have been with the company for many years. And you will ask the same question a number of times.

But… and this is a huge BUT… Yes! it is worth it. Why? Because you will have transformed the company which may have been struggling to compete, slow in its responsiveness, and wasting huge amounts on long-winded processes and old technology. You may have had a high employee churn rate or been losing market share and maybe even customers, to now being a high-performing organisation that is nimble, agile and responsive. Your organisation now becomes the place where people enjoy coming to work, they can compete at the highest level, become profitable once again, and most of all, the company is set up for a long and prosperous future, fully prepared for when the next major change in working practice comes along which could be a decade from now!

I will finish up by reiterating the point of the whole book – it is only possible with <u>YOU</u> leading the way.

A Case Study of Agile in Marketing Communications at Agicom, a leading communications company.

Strategy of Marketing Communications (MC) – The Context

In 2020, the marketing communications division of Agicom was taken over by Maria Philips, boasting a successful career in data driven personalisation and value optimisation. Her senior leadership team's mission was soon set out. To transform the world of marketing communications at Agicom and to become completely data driven and personalised across their entire base. They had to move away from historic practices of communicating with customers and potential customers, to be much closer to understanding needs and behaviours. They understood very quickly that in order to achieve this, they had to transform the division to become an Agile organisation, therefore focussing their teams on providing continuous value and be responsive to change at pace.

Agile practice was not a new concept to Agicom. They have tried to embrace it and adapt across various pockets of the business over the past few years or so. But changing a global organisation with a large town sized employee base would always take considerable time, energy, commitment and will. And in fairness, the world isn't going to hang around waiting.

Their Initial Approach

With over 400 employees and another 100 or so contractors, making the change was not going to be easy. The senior leadership team spent time drawing out the existing structure of the division and set out plans to transform into two main areas; Communications and Enablement. The teams in Communications would be very much customer facing, homing in on the journeys that customers take in the buying process, providing personalised communications to its base, and split by product and customer type. Enablement teams would provide the support and capability for the Communications teams to be able to become much more personalised and effective in its marketing.

They put every member of staff on a 3-day Agile training course over the period of about 4 weeks. Once trained the teams would be formed and up and running. There were three major drawbacks, however:

1. The transformation could not happen based on training alone. They needed proper expertise and support. They soon realised that they needed to bring in a team of coaches to help guide the teams on the ground.
2. The workload demands and expectations did not reduce sufficiently enough to allow the teams to change their ways of working, their culture, and also settle into a working arrangement in a brand-new structure. What was possible beforehand, now became far more of a challenge.
3. The Scrum Master role, tasked with focussing on helping the team to become high performing, was given as an add on set of responsibilities to an existing role within the squad, and therefore the new SMs really struggled in the beginning in being able to build their level of competency, they simply had too much to do.

Each of these 3 major impediments caused a slow progression of the adoption of Agile change in the early months. They lost some people, and the benefits of Agile implementation were not truly being felt. In addition to this, Agicom was going through a major rebranding. A mammoth project that would put great additional strain on the entire operation.

But as all good leadership teams do, they persevered. Determined to get it right, understanding that the bumps in the road were simply growing pains, or perhaps change pains. That the vision of transforming marketing communications would be realised, and that it would be revolutionary.

Both myself and the team of coaches were spread across multiple teams and were able to help support in some aspect, we focussed our efforts on building the capability of some teams, to help others. We raised and escalated systemic issues, with guidance and recommendations to senior leadership.

However, our efforts were not as effective as they could be. In order for us to truly support the change, we had to zone in on one specific area of MC and help construct a model that could be scaled across the whole division.

Intervention and New Strategy – The Customer Personalisation Alliance

About a year into the transformation, I had a long call with Mark Jennings. Head of Personalisation at Agicom. I'd spoken with Mark on a few occasions and each time he has poured out his soul to me; Frustrations, anxiety, all the issues going on in his world, a real sense of being overwhelmed. Since the big change, things had just gotten worse. His entire team had become so spread across the entire division, there were more silos than there were before, the team structure just wasn't working for them, plus everyone seemed to be constantly in meetings...I really could go on, but you get the picture. It appeared to me that both Mark and his team were at breaking point.

Personalisation is the largest area of Marketing Communications, it boasts about 1/5th of all employees and contractors. They provide enablement for not just Communication teams to help with creating personalised decisions, but also commercial trading teams and contact centres in identifying the best offers for their customers. To put it bluntly, Personalisation is a big deal, and pivotal in the overall success of the division.

I asked Mark to bring together his leadership team and let's try and dig into some of these problems to try and establish the scale of the problem here. We got together about a week later with a whiteboard and mapped out some of the key issues – only about 4 were able to make it, but enough to work with. I facilitated them through a process of root cause analysis. It was the first time that the team had really taken the time to rise above the parapet in over a year.

After a few calls we decided to get everyone in the leadership team together and flesh out a plan and strategy to not only restructure but restart, reset, renew.

That single day in London set the scene for a complete transformation of Personalisation. We even came up with a new name; The Customer Personalisation Alliance. Or "CPA" for short.

There was a considerable desire to make this work. I usually find there is some resistance or negativity in the room, perhaps a sense of fear or doubt, maybe that they have already given up. But with this group, it was different, and I have to say remained the same pretty much throughout. Something that I noticed, and it was very subtle. Everyone was on the same page, everyone was pulling in the same direction. And it was powerful. A 'can-do" attitude. A sense that now is the time, let's do this.

The three key areas identified as essential (though limited) for MC during the transformation mentioned earlier; coaching support, workload reduction and control, and dedicated roles, became the key areas we would focus on ensuring as a commitment to making this a success.

The re-structuring of the teams meant that existing development teams, some that were in excess of 20 people, were split into manageable sizes of no more than 9. Making sure there was a dedicated Scrum Master and Product Owner for each. We managed to get buy-in, acceptance and commitment from Senior Leadership, as well as stakeholders that the workload would heavily decrease down to 50% delivery for a period of 3 months. This would give each team and leadership a real opportunity to learn, settle and develop Agile knowledge and expertise. And each team grouping was given a coach to support their development.

We brought the Alliance together for an offsite kick off day. Over 100 people came. It was an opportunity to communicate the new structure and the plan, but also a chance for everyone to have their say and be heard in how things could be shaped. A chance for people to get to know one another. A chance for people to air their grievances. A chance to draw a line on the problems of yesterday and look for a new beginning starting tomorrow. The messaging was clear from Mark, "we don't have all the answers, but bear with us, work with us, and we will get there together".

For me, it was a strong message. And I could see the difference in the faces of everyone in the place. I could also see the change in Mark. He was no longer overwhelmed, anxious. But a weight had lifted from him. He was buoyant, energised, and most of all he really believed in what we were trying to do. And this too was evident on every nodding, smiling face in the room.

Following that day we entered a brief transition period, allowing for the old work to be completed and the teams to form. Every single member of the Customer Personalisation Alliance, including the leadership team, were put on an Agile training course refresher. Scrum Masters and Product Owners were given dedicated training and then embarked on a 12-week mentorship programme to help develop their competency levels.

We set up a Team of Teams. This group would help support each of the teams within the Alliance, with leadership representation from Product, Technical and Operations – The Three Amigos. Scrum Masters from each of the teams would get together with the Three Amigos regularly to escalate any impediments and align on the work across the Alliance. We needed to change the culture from hiding the bad news, to not only surfacing it, but taking ownership of the problem across CPA.

Before we properly kicked off the new structure, we got together again for an offsite day for everyone. This time was focussed on planning for the next quarter. The difference in attitude, focus and energy was striking. Maybe it was that change really was starting from the top, and despite some reservations from some on the ground, they soon got into a more positive mindset because they were following their leaders, and it was ok.

Success Measures

The Customer Personalisation Alliance are operating much more effectively and efficiently now. The teams on the ground are empowered to make decisions, to push back even. The leadership team are in full control of everything and the cultural shift, where problems are surfaced and there is a mechanism to deal with them is fully evident. They will hit bumps in the road, as is normal. But they are now in a much stronger position to drive real personalised value to their customers.

The framework that helped them to transform can now be scaled across the rest of Marketing Communications, and beyond.

Glossary of Terms

Agile

Agile uses a continual approach to building products and delivering services. Rather than focusing on the perfect end product, an Agile team delivers work in small increments. Work is continuously evaluated making teams responsive and adaptable to change. Agile is not a Project Management tool but an entire way of thinking.

Scrum

Scrum is an Agile framework that allows you to approach work in an Agile way. While Agile is about a set of principles, Scrum is the actual framework for getting the work done.

Kanban

Kanban is a Work Management system that helps teams to visualise their work and to manage their workload. Teams use Kanban Boards, where they can easily see what stage items of work are at, and Kanban Cards, which show what items of work need to be completed.

Waterfall

Waterfall is a linear Project Management process where end goals and deliverables are established at the very beginning, reverse engineered and set out in a fixed end-to-end workflow. It does not allow the same level of flexibility as Agile.

Business Agility

Business Agility is the ability of the organisation and its teams to be responsive and adapt to change at pace.

Scrum Master

A Scrum Master is a member of an Agile Scrum Team with the sole objective of helping the team towards becoming high-performing. The Scrum Master will coach, facilitate, and help the team focus and continuously improve on its ways of working together.

Kanban Lead

A Kanban Lead is a member of an Agile Kanban Team whose sole objective is to help the team towards becoming high-performing. The Kanban Lead will coach, facilitate, and help the team focus and continuously improve on its ways of working together.

Product Owner

A Product Owner is a member of an Agile Scrum or Kanban Team and will represent the needs of the customer; playing key conduit between the team and its end users. The Product Owner will define the requirements of the customer and help prioritise against business objectives and customer needs.

Value Streams

Value Streams are a concept in the structure of Agile organisations based on the flow of value from inception through to the customer. Agile Organisations set up Value Streams with an emphasis on streamlining the route from the two endpoints and ensuring the flow is short and rapid.

User Stories

A User Story is a work item (not a task) which focuses the team to look through the lens from the user's perspective, identify a problem to solve, and, by solving it, determine how it will help them.

Epics

An Epic is simply a large piece of work which is too big to bring into a sprint and requires breaking it down into small User Stories to ensure delivery of the highest value within the allotted time frame.

Bugs / Defects

In software development, a bug / defect is considered something that does not produce the expected result or intent of the User Story. This could be an error or fault. Outside of software development, it could be considered a scuff mark on a product or a spelling error on a document for example.

Product Backlog

The Product Backlog contains a prioritised list of User Stories and other work items attributed to the Agile team responsible for delivering value. The Product Backlog is maintained by the Product Owner, ensuring it is always stocked up, refined and ready for the work to begin.

Lean

The practice of Lean is a set of principles or ways of working where the onus is on streamlining efficiencies and minimising waste in processes and workflow steps. In doing so, organisations are able to focus their efforts on enhancing quality standards and becoming more responsive to change.

Lean Systems Thinking

Systems Thinking is a concept of Lean in which each part of the system is broken down into component parts, with a view to identifying how each part impacts the system. The art of Systems Thinking is to identify improvements that can be made which streamline towards becoming an optimised system.

Scrumban

It is becoming increasingly popular in modern Agile teams to operate with both main Agile frameworks of Scrum and Kanban in the management of the work. Therefore, this approach combines the benefits of discipline and the short-term focus of Scrum, combined with the gains of the fluid and adaptable workflow system focus of the Kanban process.

Scrum of Scrums (Team of Teams)

Having a Team of Teams brings representation (generally Scrum Masters and Product Owners) of multiple teams together, alongside leadership, to align on the work, escalate any impediments, and solve common problems existing at team level. The frequency of these events can vary depending on the level of problems that need solving. Once again, this is not a progress update meeting.

Sprints

In Scrum, work is split into a timebox called Sprints. These Sprints reduce risks as changes can be implemented quickly and keep everyone motivated with short bursts of activity, with the onus on delivering value at the end.

Sprint Planning

At the beginning of each sprint, the Scrum Team will get together to plan the sprint. The Product Owner will set out the objectives (sprint goals) to be achieved and the team will plan tasks against each User Story that will go into the sprint to achieve the goal.

Daily Stand-Up

Each day, an Agile Scrum or Kanban team will gather around the team board to align on the work, and raise/escalate any impediments to progress. This event is scheduled for 15 minutes and is sufficient time for alignment to take place. It is not a progress meeting. It is called a Stand-Up as it is proven that people struggle to stand beyond 15 minutes and therefore the onus is on the efficiency of a short burst of communication.

Burndown Chart

The Burndown Chart shows the ideal line from the beginning to the end of the sprint. It provides a real-time view of how the team are getting on each day with a view to acting if necessary to get on track.

Sprint Review

At the end of each sprint, the team will gather to review how they have succeeded against the sprint goals. The Scrum Master will show the team a picture of the sprint using the final Burndown Chart and how this sprint compares to previous sprints in terms of average capability. The team will then showcase the work delivered. Stakeholders are encouraged to attend the review to provide feedback on User Stories ready for delivery.

Retrospective

After the review, the team only (not including stakeholders) will gather to reflect on the sprint. This is an opportunity for each member to highlight (typically) what went well, and what didn't go quite as planned and come up with ideas on how the team can improve on its way of working in the next sprint. These improvement suggestions will go into the next Sprint Planning to ensure the team are continuously improving and working towards a state of high performance.

Story Points

In Agile practice, teams will use Story Points as a means to estimate the work. These are typically based on three factors – complexity, effort and risk, and follow the following sequence: 0.5, 1, 2, 3, 5, 8, 13, 20. The team will estimate together as a cross-functional team and these can then be used to discuss the work, as well as assist in planning the capability of the team in a sprint once an average of how many Story Points are delivered over 2-3 sprints and beyond.

Cycle Time

The Cycle Time is used in Kanban practice and is a measurement to help teams identify the length of time a work item takes to move through the Kanban workflow system (board). It is used to help identify delays in the system and also the capability of the team.

Lead Time

The Lead Time is used in Kanban practice and is a measurement to help teams identify the length of time a work item spends in the backlog before moving through the system and then through to being completed. It is used to help provide clarity on delivery estimates.

Kaizen

In Agile practice, teams are encouraged to make small changes each day for continuous improvements in how they operate. In Japan, this is called Kaizen.

About the Author

STEVE MARTIN is the CEO and founder of agile coaching company Agilistic.

A certified Enterprise Agile Coach, Steve has supported C-suite leaders and management teams in transforming their organisations into highly efficient and effective companies, helping them to become more adaptable and responsive to their customers' needs, and transforming their culture and working practices to become more agile.

Steve has worked with a wide variety of organisations including BT, Vodafone, HM Revenue & Customs, William Hill and The Department for Environment, Food and Rural Affairs.